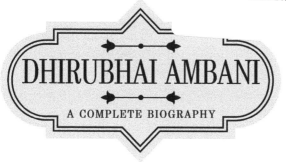

DHIRUBHAI AMBANI

A COMPLETE BIOGRAPHY

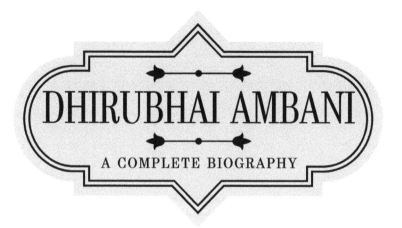

DHIRUBHAI AMBANI

A COMPLETE BIOGRAPHY

N. CHOKKAN

PRABHAT PAPERBACKS

Published by
PRABHAT PAPERBACKS
An imprint of Prabhat Prakashan Pvt. Ltd.
4/19 Asaf Ali Road,
New Delhi-110002 (INDIA)
e-mail: prabhatbooks@gmail.com

ISBN 978-93-5521-398-3
DHIRUBHAI AMBANI A COMPLETE BIOGRAPHY
by N. Chokkan

Edition
First, 2023

to my dear friend and guide
Srikanth Meenakshi

Author's Note

Our beloved former President A.P.J. Abdul Kalam once said, "A dream is not what you see while asleep, it is those thoughts that do not let you sleep." It is time to make these words your life philosophy.

There was a person in India who has taken Kalam's words as his life's motto half a century ago and has never failed to follow it in each step of his life. He has made his life's dream come true through his hard work and has raised to the peak – He is Dhirubhai Ambani!

A popular Tamil song written by Pattukottaiyar says, "Do not fret about poverty, neither forget that you have skills". If a person possesses the skills along with the ability to dream big for his future, he can reach insurmountable heights and Dhirubhai Ambani's success story proves this.

Ambani was born in Gujarat, he started his business in Mumbai, and was successful in his ventures. His success story is not as popular among the South Indians as it is among the North Indians.

But, Ambani is a famous person irrespective of the state he belong to. He can be proclaimed as an example of self-made man. If a person who did not have any prior experience or proper guidance has overcome every obstacle that life has thrown on his way and has reached the pinnacle, then there should be 'something' that could be learned from his life, isn't that right?

This book will try to define and explain that 'something' to its readers!

I convey my heartfelt thanks to my dear friend Pa. Raghavan who wanted me to write a complete biography of Dhirubhai Ambani in Tamil and English language!

I thank my beloved friend Angaraiyan who generously helped me to procure the information required for this book. I am also deeply indebted to Icarus Prakash who patiently clarified all my doubts regarding the business world. Thank you both for your support!

When I start writing, I become a non-present member of the family despite being present in the house. Although I realize that it is not a good practice, I still haven't mastered the art of balancing both. I thank my loving wife Uma for tolerating my absence and for supporting me!

Ambani himself has once said that "A single Ambani is not enough for India, it needs thousands like me!" If this book helps to make one another Ambani, I would be elated.

With love,

N. Chokkan,
Bengaluru.

Contents

Chapter 1

It was the day when the big boss was scheduled to visit. Hence, all who were present in that advertising company were amped up for the visit.

The person who was about to visit them was not an ordinary person, he was the one who was the incharge of the huge management. Starting from the colors and designs of the export apparel, right to the wheat flour used in their canteen for rotis, he expected purity and high quality. He never hesitated to point out mistakes, and at the same time, he appreciated a job done well.

Within his organization, every decision, be it small or big will progress only after his approval. If he was not satisfied with the work, then it had to be done repeatitively until it met his expectations, irrespective of the number of attempts taken to meet his expectations. He never compromised on quality; he was unyielding until the quality he aspired is met.

That boss was visiting the advertising department that day. A few important magazine advertisements were prepared the previous day. If the boss comes in and approves it, everybody can release their bated breath. If not, they have to start the work again from the scratch. Hence, all the employees were tense.

The boss was always on time and he arrived as usual. He inquired about the well-being of everybody with genuine care. He immersed himself in the advertisement proofs which were kept on his desk.

A few pressure-filled minutes passed by. Boss's silence came to an end at last. He started with appreciation, "Very good, all the designs have come out well!" He gave his approval with a few minute corrections. He asked them to send the advertisement to the magazines after fixing those few corrections.

The advertisement team thanked him feeling relieved and proud. He thanked them too and after a few handshakes, he was ready to leave.

A young employee who was one among the advertising team then came before him. He wanted to say something but was hesitant. The boss understood his hesitation and asked, 'What is the matter, sir?'. He had the humble habit of addressing everyone from the peon to the officers as 'Sir'.

"I want to give you a suggestion, sir" before he could complete his sentence, murmurs started to arise from the back. Everyone was silenced by the boss's stare. "Yes, sir, tell me what do you want to suggest?"

The young man swallowed his fear and spoke, "Sir, I am working in this marketing department for the last four years. Since we are creating several advertisements for our company's products, we work here actively. But…"

"But?" The young man was scared of looking at the boss' sneer. Yet he continued, "I feel that utilizing this skilled marketing group for creating advertisements for our company alone is not enough, sir. Each one of us working here is a creative person, but if we were asked to create only textile advertisements daily, then we will not have a chance to utilize our talents to their full extent."

The boss's face shrunk learning this. Murmurs started to rise again from the backside. All were scared if their cushy job was in danger.

Which boss will like if an employee is not satisfied with the company which gives him proper salary and other benefits and then he stubbornly asks for creativity?

But, this boss did like the suggestion. He patted the young man on his shoulder and smiled. "What you say is right, sir. I know it is tough for you creative people to do the same job daily. What do you want to do? I am sure you have some plans?"

The young man breathed easily and smiled. "Yes, sir. I wanted to talk to you regarding that today' he said enthusiastically. 'What if we change this company to a public advertising agency or a marketing group which can be used to make advertisements for all the paying companies and not only for us?"

Boss's approval of the idea was evident in his continued smile, "That is a good suggestion, we can do it. Your talents will be well utilized then" he said. He said, "Start immediately to form a new advertising agency, you can make all the arrangements needed for it. I will provide my support and our company will be the first customer of that advertising agency!"

Everybody including the young man was astonished. How can a person be so reasonable and give his blessings when his employee, who gets his salary from him and who works in his office accounts him for the lack of wholesome work!

Is he an ordinary person? He was the one who started a spinning mill with just four machines and conquered the export business. He was the one who introduced polyester clothes in the local market and gained huge fame and profits. His company's clothing and his company's shares were selling like hot cakes all over India. The World Bank and a few foreign magazines visited his spinning mills and have given their 'A+' certificate!

What might be the reason for such a person to listen and encourage the ideas of an ordinary young man who was working for him?

There can be only one reason – he clearly understood that all his growth started from a tiny point! He did not forget his roots no matter how high he has reached! He still remembered his struggle when he was of the young man's age and was knocking at closed doors with innovative ideas and new suggestions. So, he was able to understand the thirst of that young man who was bubbling to 'achieve something new and big'.

Soon after that, the advertising department was dissolved and a new agency named 'Mudra communications' was born. The advice given to its managers by the boss can be shortly said as his life's essence, "No matter whichever field you choose, work hard to achieve something greater than all those who have worked on that particular field have achieved so far. Dream big and work hard to achieve it!"

'Mudra Communications', which was separated from a huge enterprise, which had its old boss as its first (and only) customer, which was launched in a tiny room in Mumbai has now grown into one of the top five advertising agencies of India! ("I Love you Rasna", one of the popular advertisements which is still sung by kids of this age is one of their creations!)

Mudra's founder A.G. Krishnamoorthy won the lifetime achievement award in the field of advertising in 1999. In his acceptance speech at the award ceremony, he commended his 'Boss' who gave him the confidence and opportunity. "The trust he has in his employees is the first and foremost reason for the achievements made by Mudra and me today!"

That Boss was the one who gave the confidence to each Indian through his hard work and success that if we dream without sleeping, if we work toward that dream without giving up, if we keep on going in our journey, tremendous victories can be easily won. He was 'Dhirajlal Hirachand Ambani' who is popularly known as 'Dhirubhai Ambani'!

Just like poetry which has two kinds—classical and contemporary poetry, there are two kinds in entrepreneurs too – classical entrepreneurs and new entrepreneurs!

The first kind is those who are born into this world with the comforts of wealth earned by their fathers and grandfathers. Those who are born with a silver spoon, grow up with all the comforts and high-class education. Once they complete their education either within India or in foreign countries, they take charge of their company at a young age. They become a boss through their pedigree. After that, according to their talents, they either increase, decrease or maintain the wealth collected by their ancestors!

A new entrepreneurs' world is entirely different, most of them are born in either middle-class or low-class families. Due to their underdeveloped economy, most of the people surrounding them will be satisfied with short-term goals like mediocre education, government salary, dowry (without police problem), children, retirement with benefits, Kasi visit within their lifetime, and a trouble-free death. In between them, a few misfits get the idea to start something new somehow. They lose interest in getting a salary from others and aim to give a salary to others. They roam around and struggle to get a small business loan from the government or banks, start a small-scale industry, and get satisfied. If they are not exhausted with that, they might achieve something after that. If the flame inside them continues to burn, they can achieve a lot more!

While comparing the classical entrepreneurs to the new ones, the new entrepreneurs often lack luck. The money, education, and comforts which the classical entrepreneurs get without any strain can be obtained by the new ones only after a huge struggle. Their achievement is minimized by the struggle!

But, many new entrepreneurs have managed to throw away these calculations and rules and they have achieved high. Dhirubhai Ambani can be quoted as an example of such an entrepreneur. He was born in a small village in Gujarat as a son of a poor teacher. His education was stopped at an early age due to poverty and he started as a child laborer. He utilized his talents and dreams as his investments and fought against all odds to raise himself as one of the biggest entrepreneurs of India!

Dhirubhai Ambani's native place is Chorwad in Gujarat. He was born on December 28, 1932. His father Hirachand Gordhandas was a teacher in the local school. He was the third son of his mother Jamna Ben. He had four siblings – two brothers and two sisters.

Hirachand Gordhadas was known as a strict teacher in the village. But since his meager income was insufficient, poverty danced in his house. He managed to send his children to school despite his hardship.

Dhirubhai Ambani was an average student. Math evaded him mercilessly. Since his friend Jivabhai Rathod was there to teach him Math, Ambani managed to pass each class in school.

Dhirubhai was an obedient son at home. He was known to do all the household activities which other kids refuse to do. Apart from this, due to the family's poverty, he was running a business during his weekends!

In general, Gujarati people are known for their business-trade skills. Dhirubhai was no exception to this belief, he realized his responsibility and spent his free time helping with his family's finances.

A sacred place named 'Girnar hill' was near to his village. Since ancient Hindu and Jain temples were located on that hill, devotees visit the hill in groups from faraway places. Ambani realized that the devotees expected tasty food on their trip and thus he started to sell tasty snacks downhill.

He did not earn much in that venture. But, it was true that he had earned the ability to utilize an opportunity laid before him, the skill to understand the nuances of trade on his own and someone he halso had the thirst to earn more at an early age!

It was the time when the freedom struggle was at its peak. Ambani and his friends who were a part of their school's NCC team wanted to do something. But they were not clear on what to do.

In that situation, police arrested one of Ambani's friends who participated in a riot. He was charged with triggering a religious riot case and was sent to prison.

Ambani was confident that his friend did not commit any crime. So, he gathered a few supporters and went to the police station. He started protesting against the policemen to release his friend!

Police tried to subdue the protest somehow. They tried all possible ways. Nothing worked against Ambani. They even threatened to arrest him, but Ambani did not waver and continued his protest. At last, the police gave away and released his friend!

The situation at Ambani's house and school was rebellious too. Dhirubhai Ambani who managed to pass the regular tests with difficulty failed in his tenth standard public examination. He was able to pass the tenth standard only on his second attempt.

But, what is the use in passing the tenth standard? Who had the money to educate him further?

Owing to unyielding poverty, Ambani's education ended with the tenth standard.

What next? He had to find a job for himself just like all the young men who completed their education or stopped their education halfway!

Ambani started searching for jobs within his village, but nothing was available. So he went to Mumbai and started searching for jobs. But, that did not work out too. While he was wondering what to do next, he received support from an unexpected direction.

Although Dhirubhai was an average student, his sense of responsibility has attracted many in his village. A few of them genuinely wanted to help that young man who wanted to reduce the burden of his family. One of them suggested a plan to Dhirubhai, 'Your brother works in Yeden, right? Why don't you join him there and start to work?'

Although it was a good idea, Ambani was not interested in it initially, "Who will be ready to employee me there?"

'Do not worry about that, I will make arrangements for that' the well-wisher said. He further asked, 'Are you ready to leave India and go to Yeden? Will you be able to leave everybody here and work hard there?'

'I can!' Confidence and eagerness shone in the seventeen-year-old Ambani's eyes, "No matter which country or distance, I can go and I will go!"

When Dhirubhai Ambani said he accepted to go, it was his eagerness to solve his family's poverty that triggered him. But, apart from everything else, he had the confidence that although he had to leave then, he would come back to his land and achieve something big.

❏

Chapter 2

Today's gulf country 'Yemen' was known as 'Yeden' then. Although it was under the British colonialism, the tiny nation had huge popularity due to its oil resource and the import-exports between several countries including England and Australia through its harbours!

In addition to this, all the ships which passed through Yeden used to halt in its harbour, stay for a few days, fill their fuel tanks, complete the minor repair works needed on the craft, and only then did they depart from the country. Hence, several businesses and trades flourished depending on their harbour and those who visit them.

Although Yeden was an Arab country, several companies employed Indians in their firms. In particular, the Gujarati population was more. Most of them had left their native place in search of a livelihood!

Dhirubhai Ambani's brother Ramnikbhai had already left for Yeden and was working in a petroleum company. So, when Dhirubhai wanted to go there, his family were not too worried. But they sent him off with parting tears while wishing him luck!

They did not have any other option. The patriarch of their house Hirachand Ambani had died recently and hence young members of the family were forced to bear the family burden.

Is it enough, when a decision to go to Yeden is made? With God's grace and with neighbours' blessings he got a job recommendation in Yeden. But, what about the expenses to reach there? Shouldn't he buy a few good dresses to wear? Shouldn't he have some money for travel? Shouldn't he have to pay for the tickets to travel by a ship?

Ambani, who had never seen a hundred rupee note so far was fretting about how to get the money. God decided to help him under the disguise of Ambani's neighbour Surababa Bharta.

Ambani received Bharta's money gratefully and pledged to return the amount as soon as possible. Not only did Ambani returned the amount within a short period after reaching Yeden, but he also gave jobs to Bharta's son and grandson in his company—Reliance. A help in need is a help indeed, isn't it right?

A few other relatives and family friends extended their help and Dhirubhai Ambani was ready to travel to Yeden soon!

When Ambani traveled in a ship named 'Kabota' buying the cheapest ticket available, he was only seventeen – it was during the year 1949!

After reaching Yeden, Ambani joined a small trading company. But what job might be waiting for him who had studied just up to the tenth standard? He was helping the owner and was doing petty jobs for the other employees. His salary was 125 rupees in Indian value!

There is no surprise in Dhirubhai Ambani hating that job, who was hunting for challenges right from a young age. He started to look for better jobs in Yeden itself!

Dhirubhai's brother Ramnikbhai was working for a French trading company named 'A. Besse & Co'. Through his recommendation, Dhirubhai also joined the same company in its petroleum division.

Royal Dutch Shell was the name of the division that employed Dhirubhai Ambani then. They were the wholesale sellers of the famous 'Shell' group then. Ambani joined as a petrol bunk helper in the division that was selling Shell's petroleum products in Yeden. His salary was three hundred rupees.

Although his salary has increased by two folds from his previous job, there was no improvement in the nature of work done by Ambani. He was employed to fill petrol for the harbour vehicles!

The menial job gave monotony to the active youngster, Ambani. But, Ambani differed from his peers in that point. Instead of complaining about his 'monotonous' work, he started to observe the operations of the mega-company that was running around him. He observed everybody including all the managers, assistant managers, employees, supervisors, and noted down his observations. He questioned himself about why did they do their task in this way and not the other way and answered his own questions. The obscurity about why a petrol bunk helper would need to know such information, helped him to efficiently manage his own company!

A small example can be given for his strategy – while he was thinking twice to spend ten rupees, Ambani could not believe that his company was spending more than five thousand rupees just to send a telegram. Why should so much amount be spent on sending a telegram? He calculated the amount that can be saved by avoiding telegrams!

But, at the same time, when he understood that the company might get lakhs and crores of profit or loss based on the information sent through the telegram, he understood everything. If he tries to avoid a five thousand rupees' expenditure, he might face a huge loss. So, he learned the important lesson that he should not be stingy in important matters and should spend money when required.

Ambani felt that he was attending a school each day he worked for Shell. He understood that there were many life lessons to be learned in that huge organization if he stayed vigilant instead of lazing around.

While looking at everything that happened around him, a secret desire bloomed in his heart, "I will start and run such a huge organization one day" he said to himself. "My company will also dig petroleum from oil wells, purify it and export it to the world around!"

It is normal for a villager to look at a candy factory with awe. It is somewhat rare for a villager to observe and learn about the products manufactured in a candy factory and the way it was prepared. But, how about the same villager aspiring to start a candy factory by himself?

That is Ambani! He never lacked in the conviction of his dreams, he never lost his confidence in himself to make that dream come true. This attitude made the young man who was filling petrol for a paltry monthly salary imagine himself to be the owner of a petroleum company. It also made him transform his dreams into a reality at a later stage!

It was not just his dream which drove Ambani, but also his confidence that "if they can do it, I can also do it!" which differentiated him from the rest of the crowd.

A small incident is cited as an example of Ambani's bravery and his courage to face hazards.

Goods were being boarded in one of the ships belonging to 'Shell'. Ambani and his friends completed their tasks and were taking a rest on the top floor of the ship. The time was around midnight.

One among them pointed at the harbor which was shining brightly and asked playfully, 'Who can swim to the shore?'

Everyone around him looked at each other without uttering anything. There was a reason for their hesitation – the ship was anchored at a distance from the harbour. If one had to swim from the ship to the shore, he had to swim more than a kilometer – in the dark!

Moreover, the sea surrounding Yeden harbour was known for its sharks. Can one risk his life for the sake of a dare?

Since everybody was silent, the person who asked the question was irritated. "Why is that nobody uttering a word? Is anybody ready for the challenge?" he asked loudly.

The word 'challenge' triggered Ambani. He raised quickly from his place and faced the person who offered the challenge, "I will swim to the shore, want to bet?" he asked.

On hearing his words, everybody was shocked. They advised Ambani that it was not a wise decision to swim among the sharks during nighttime.

But, Ambani did not consider their advice. There was no second thinking in his mind after deciding to cross the distance. He asked the person, 'What do I get if swim across?'

He replied after thinking, 'One ice cream'.

All the surrounding members laughed at the prize offered. They made fun of the prize offered for the risk.

But, Ambani did not falter. He showed thumbs up accepting the challenge, stripped off his shirt, and jumped into the water immediately!

While his friends were standing shocked, Ambani crossed the distance and won the ice cream. The midnight ice cream would have been extra tasty for him that day!

The point to be noted in this incident is that, although he was aware of the risk involved, Ambani trusted his skill and took a calculated risk. This courage of him enabled him to dream big at an early age and drove him toward his goals!

The owner of the 'Shell' company in which Ambani was employed in Yeden was a Jew. He noticed Dhirubhai Ambani observing several things around him including management, trade and money. He also noticed Ambani asking questions around him and understanding everything. He was impressed by Ambani's interest and his energy. He enquired about Ambani and promoted him from petrol pump duty to a delivery clerk!

Challenges and opportunities to learn were more at the new job! Since Ambani was yearning for both, he worked hard utilizing all his talents. Very soon, he rose to the position of supervising all the tasks of the company from loading and unloading goods in ships and aircraft!

Ambani involved himself in all the activities during his free time. One among them was helping his friends with problems related to insurance – that is, applying to the concerned insurance companies, if needed he debated with them and got the amount. He took a certain percentage of that amount as his salary and hence he was able to earn more!

Ambani had the habit of utilizing his free time effectively. He read English newspapers regularly to improve his English and world knowledge. He started learning the local Arabic language and soon started to speak to them fluently!

During that time, he found a good friend named Pravinbhai Thakkar!

Thakkar was also from Gujarat who came to Yeden to search for his livelihood. His brother was running a shop named Popular Stores near Yeden harbour. Thakkar joined his brother in the shop.

Thakkar was introduced to Ambani by his elder brother Ramnikbhai. They both became close friends soon. To be specific, it was Thakkar who identified the passion, dreams and goals which were simmering in Ambani's eyes.

Pravinbhai Thakur who was working in his brother's shop so far started a new shop in 1953. Its name was 'Reliance Stores', Thakkar obtained the selling rights from popular companies like Rolex and Canon and started running his shop in full swing.

Thakkar had Ambani's complete support for his bold move. While Ambani was immersed in his dreams of starting a business all by himself and not to be employed anymore, the bold move taken by his friend was inspiring to him. He encouraged Thakkar's attempts.

He liked the name 'Reliance' especially as it meant trusting somebody. A person who does trade relies on his customers always. It looked like the name emphasizes that customers are God for a business person. He thought to himself that no other name can perfectly fit a business organization.

Pravinbhai Thakkar's new store gained popularity soon. It brought him name and fame. Thakkar bought a Mercedes car using the profit from the store. When he showed it to Ambani, Ambani hugged his friend with overwhelming happiness, 'Reliance has brought you luck!'

That was the moment when Ambani started to love the name 'Reliance'. He was enthralled by the name's match and the luck it brought. Due to his fascination with the name, when he started a business on his own, Ambani named it 'Reliance'!

While he was in Yeden, Ambani spent each second in dreaming and planning for his future. At the same time, he completed all the tasks assigned to him in the petroleum company and earned a good name!

But small victories and accolades were not enough to quench his thirst. The desire to achieve something big was flaming inside him. After looking at his friend Pravinbhai's entry into trade and finding success in it, Ambani's desire amplified several times. He had to do something. But, when?

Ambani did not bother about the question "How?", since he had the confidence to do anything, his main question was "When?' – When will I overcome the comfort of doing what was expected and getting a monthly salary without any risks or worries? When will I grow into somebody who employs others?

With these questions in his mind, five years after reaching Yeden, Ambani returned to India in 1954 for a vacation. His family had made marriage arrangements for him then. He married Kokilaben and returned to Yeden with her.

Ambani's dreams and desire to earn more increased several folds after marriage. But, at the same time, he was confused by another thought.

It was the same question that almost all the middle-class people who go abroad to earn get – How long should I live here? When will I decide that what I have earned is enough and return to my homeland?

The petrol company treated Ambani well. He was promoted to Marketing Manager at a young age (24) and was given a good salary. But, Ambani's wish was not only a monthly salary!

Ambani made several calculations based on his dreams and his family's future – his heart wanted to return to his homeland and start a business. But he reached Yeden to earn for his family and he was not ready to return without doing it properly. Moreover, he had just begun his own family then.

Moreover, even if he returned to India, how would he get the capital to start a business? While thinking about everything, he concluded – he fixed a target amount for himself, so, until he saves that amount, he has to live in Yeden and after that, he can go back to his home place. He decided to face his fate in India after that!

Ambani, who joined at three hundred rupees' monthly salary was earning around thousand two hundred rupees then. He calculated that if he managed to save an amount regularly, he can go back to India within a few years.

But he found a route soon through his sharp intelligence and observation. It was a murky route, but an honest one.

Chapter 3

There was a sudden demand for our Indian currency a few years back. Some great-minded person started a rumor that the silver line which runs along the Indian currency notes is more valuable than the currency note itself. Many believed that rumor to be true and tried to extract that silver line to sell and failed in their attempt!

Ambani had a similar idea in Yeden. But the difference was that his idea was a genuine one. The quantity of silver in their currency was in abundance!

The currency of Yeden was 'Riyal'. Yeden people used the 'Riyal' coins which were made out of pure silver then.

But nobody had the vision to calculate the silver available in their coins!

Only Ambani had that idea – and that happened by chance!

While he was weighing the 'Riyal' coin, he calculated how much profit will he get if he sells the silver present in the coin in the England market. When he realized that the amount was greater than the actual value of the coin itself, the business tycoon inside him woke up and got ready.

We are not sure whether the government made a mistake or if the price of silver rose after the coins were issued. But, if we consider the value of the silver coin which was present in Ambani's hands as ten pounds, the market rate of the silver present in that coin was higher than ten pounds, much higher!

Ambani found his opportunity in that difference. He did not reveal his discovery and started to collect Riyal coins. He melted those coins, changed them into silver blocks and started to sell them to England's silver agents. He found considerable profit in that venture!

Could he rest after knowing that his plan was earning huge profits? As the next stage, he started to buy silver coins from his friends and co-workers at a price. He paid them in currency notes for the coins and was melting their coins.

This interesting 'coin' game lasted for three months. It is said that the government found about it and got back their Riyal coins. Ambani earned a lot within that time in his new business!

Some people are awed by this cleverness and opportunity-hunting nature of Ambani and there are people who claim that melting coins is illegal. But, both of them should accept the fact that Ambani was clever enough to make use of an opportunity that was given to him. All the people who were in Yeden had the same silver coin in their hands, but nobody thought of calculating its real worth! Ambani found a mistake that was missed by that government and used it for his benefit. It can be seen as a fitting punishment to the Yeden government!

The sudden business was so profitable to Ambani that he almost reached the amount which he had targeted in his mind!

Ambani's firstborn, Mukesh was born in 1957. His passion to return to India increased after that!

We have to note something here. Before going to Yeden, Dhirubhai Ambani's family could not even be termed as middle-class. He reached Yeden as a representative of a family which was unable to bear their state of poverty in search of a livelihood. He worked hard from 1949 to 1957. He learned many new things, he joined as an office boy in a land which spoke an unknown language and raised until he became a marketing manager – everything happened before he was 25 years old!

Any other person would have been satisfied with this growth. They would have held on to this development and got saturated.

Ambani's uniqueness is portrayed here – he dared to quit a comfortable job in a foreign land which gave him ample benefits. He believed that he can succeed if he pours in the same effort which he poured into the foreign land. He took all his earnings and returned to India with his wife, children and his brother to invest his earnings and start a new business.

When Ambani was asked about it in the later days, he gave an interesting explanation. Let us look at that in his own words.

"This world consists of large circular orbits. Those orbits are located one above the other. The lowest orbit consists of peons and clerks. The highest orbit consists of leading businessmen, politicians and other successful people.

You and I are revolving somewhere in one of the orbits revolving in the middle. We are revolving in the same orbit that was given to us.

What should we do if we want to succeed in overcoming our environment? We have to break our orbit and come out of it. For that, we have to jump toward the orbit that is above us. Nobody will help us in the process. We cannot expect the people above us to pull us up. We have to try and climb up!

Once we get settled in that new orbit, we have to climb to the one above it and after some time climb up an other orbit. Until we reach the highest orbit, we have to continue this process. This is the secret of success!"

Leaving the comfort of his manager's job and a steady salary in a foreign country and entering into the 'business' orbit forms the first episode of Ambani's success history – his courage and motivation took him to great heights!

***

Nobody knew the exact savings amount that Dhirubhai Ambani had when he returned to India in 1957. Some say five hundred and some others say fifty thousand. Nobody knew the truth. But he was ready to invest everything he earned in Yeden in his new business.

He decided that industrial city Mumbai was suitable for him and shifted to Mumbai with his mother, brothers, wife and children. Their residence was a small flat in a congested area named Venilal Estates amidst the shouts and cries of clothing, jewelry and craft stores.

He has decided to start a business in Mumbai. But what business?

Ambani took some time to decide that. He visited several business centers including petty shops, huge trade companies, export companies, stock exchange and observed the people, their needs, non-needs, which product has high demand and low demand, which yielded huge profits and low profits and several other happenings. He did not know any Indian language other than Gujarati during that period!

On calculating the information obtained by observing and talking to his friends, Ambani decided to indulge himself in the export business. He planned to export Indian spices like cardamom, cloves, turmeric, ginger from India to West Asian countries since Indian spices had high demand and Ambani thought that the project would yield profit with low investment.

Ambani's export company was started in 1958 on a smaller scale. He learned the nuances of export trade by cleaning cashews and turmeric and packaging them in neat parcels.

His journey was not smooth in the early days. Most of the Indian trades were managed by a few companies and a few families in India. When a newcomer enters the market other than them, they crushed them by not providing them any support. A newcomer overcoming the hurdles posted by them and achieving something needed high endurance! Ambani understood the situation and was ready to face the challenges!

Ambani did not become a bigshot during a single night as shown in our Indian movies. His trade kingdom started in a tiny room that measured five feet on each side. His brother and he were the only employees at the beginning. Ambani stayed in that small room, monitored the market situation and calculated which product would yield him good profit and which country it should be sent to.

Since Ambani was new to the export business, he did not get the skill of deciding what to do and what not to do instantly. So, he did everything that he wanted to do without any second thoughts. This attitude might seem wrong but it became one of Ambani's strengths. He did several tasks which others hesitated and this led him through several unopened doors. He was able to sell even soil and earn money!

This is not fake, Ambani exported soil and made a profit in real!

Ambani came to know through somebody that several rich people of Arab countries wanted to grow rose plants in their houses and offices. But they could not find the soil to grow rose plants in their desert!

Ambani's business brain was activated on hearing about this information by chance. He started to select the soil that was suitable for growing rose plants and exported it to Arabian deserts! His company earned huge profits in that venture!

Ambani's export group proved that not only flowers but also trade flourishes in the Indian soil!

***

The next turning point in Ambani's life came through a government notice – the Indian government announced that cotton clothes had greater demand in African countries and announced several concessions for those who export clothes to African countries.

Ambani who was selling cardamom was interested in that. Where can he purchase cotton clothes? He started enquiring if he can buy the clothes from the weavers who weave them or from the sellers, where can he get quality clothes and the purchase rates.

While he was searching for a contact to assist him in the venture, he remembered something – the company which employed him for the first time in Yeden was involved in buying and selling clothes for a long time.

Ambani enquired if that company had any branches in Mumbai. When he approached them for help, they accepted his proposal readily as they considered Ambani as one among them!

Since Ambani had the support of a bigshot who was in the same business for several years, everything happened with full speed after that. That company introduced several owners of weaving factories to Ambani directly. Ambani made legal agreements with those owners and started to export cotton clothes to foreign countries.

That was Ambani's introduction to the textile world. He created a huge empire holding on to that single piece of thread!

Ambani decided to expand his business further in 1959, but more investment was needed for that. He included his relative Champaklal Damani (he was a Yeden return too) in his business. The new company was named 'Reliance Commercial Corporation'!

The store run by his friend Pravinbhai Thakkar in Yeden, its success and the impact it had made on Ambani made him choose the name 'Reliance'. He believed that his new company will have a blessing with the name. While talking about it, Ambani made fun that he has snatched the name from his friend.

Only the name 'Reliance' was new, but there was no change in anything that Ambani was doing earlier. Reliance was involved completely in the export trade. Ambani employed two other people to share the workload.

The funny fact was that the tiny office of Reliance could not hold four members. To give you a clear picture, apart from a table, three chairs and a telephone, not even a bell pin can be inserted into that office. So, although Reliance employed four members, only three could sit inside the office and work. Until one of them comes out, the fourth person had to stand outside the room!

Ambani was indulged in his dreams for the future in that tiny room. He was involved completely in the clothing export business then. He was eagerly waiting for opportunities in the same trade.

During that period, clothes made of manmade fiber named Synthetic were gaining popularity in India. Reliance bought the synthetic fibers needed to weave that clothes wholesale and was selling it to manufacturers and mills.

Reliance earned a decent profit in buying and selling synthetic fibers. Yet, Ambani had an incomplete feeling in his mind. He analyzed how to earn more money in that trade and found out an idea!

Not only in that trade, but his idea also brought him a good name and ample profits in evey businesses he did in the future. That idea was the one said by Tamil poet, Thiruvalluvar long back – Think big!

Ambani decided to involve himself big-time in whichever business he gets involved in. He considered selling cows was more beneficial than selling milk. While going for the bigger target, raw materials can be purchased at a lower rate and if sold properly, greater profit can be obtained!

According to this plan, while other merchants were purchasing hundred tons of synthetic fibers, Ambani's Reliance company purchased ten thousand tons of synthetic fibers at the same time. Since the price will be less for those who purchase in bulk, they got fibers at the lowest rate in the market.

But, is that enough? Only if he sells the goods purchased at low cost at a 'higher profit' his goal can be reached!

Ambani utilized all his skills and started to work hard. He traveled to each mill that manufactured synthetic clothes in Mumbai and its surrounding towns in town bus and talked to each of the mill owners. He convinced them that his synthetic fibers are the best quality in the city and only if they use them, their clothes will be well-liked!

There is no wonder that Ambani's pleasant face, smooth talk and amicable nature attracted all the owners. Moreover, since he bought the synthetic fibers at a lower rate, he was able to sell them at a lower rate when compared to the other merchants. So, they continued to buy the raw materials needed from Ambani continuously. The result was that, while other merchants struggled to sell their hundred tons of fiber, Reliance sold all the ten thousand tons of fiber and enjoyed good profits. This did not happen once or twice, but each time!

At the same time, Reliance got involved in raw materials needed for fibers and the plastic trade. Ambani had his relative Rasiklal Meswani and assistant Manubhai Seth with him during that period. The three members can be termed as the major factors for the initial growth of Reliance!

Although Ambani earned a good income through his business, his family was still residing at the old flat. There was no telephone, no car and no cot too – everybody was still sleeping on the floor.

After the birth of his first son Mukesh, Ambani had two more daughters and a son. All of Ambani's children grew up in small house, 'Venilal Estates' playing with neighboring kids and sharing their siblings' dresses and books.

The reason behind Ambani's humble residence even after earning a little was not stinginess, but responsibility. Ambani liked to be simple, always. He banned unwanted expenses not only at home but also in his office.

Ambani's policy was only one in this aspect – he never hesitated to spend lakhs or crores if he feels that something is necessary. But, at the same time, if the lack of something can be managed well, he will skip spending on it!

For example, he and his friend Murli Deora had to travel to Delhi several times officially. Although train transport was cheaper, they traveled in airplanes considering the time involved in train travel. So, Ambani used to choose the cheapest airplane available for their travel.

Their work at Delhi used to complete within a day mostly. Staying at a hotel for the short duration was an unwanted expense. But, at the same time, the people who they have to meet in Delhi were successful industrialists or government officials. If any of them asked him about his place of stay and how to contact them, what can he reply to them?

Ambani found a way for that. He made a secret agreement with an employer of the famous hotel 'Ashoka' in New Delhi.

Whenever Ambani reached Delhi, he went to the Ashoka hotel and informed about his arrival. After that, he can say that he stays in the hotel Ashoka to whomever he had to meet that day. If any of them wants to contact Ambani and calls the hotel, Ambani's person would politely say that he has gone out and receive the message. He collected all the telephonic messages received that day and handed them over to Ambani who used to visit the hotel in the evening. His one day's 'service' earned him twenty-five rupees!

Using this trick, Ambani created an image that he stays in the hotel Ashoka whenever he visits Delhi. It was not for an appearance, it was because others had a telephone number to contact Ambani and he can save a day's room rent!

Ambani saved upto a hundred and twenty rupees each time he visited Delhi through cheap air tickets and the 'Ashoka' trick. Each penny he earned by his diligence was added to the profits Reliance earned!

Due to Ambani's continuous motivation, his employees actively provided their efforts and hence Ambani's export and other local businesses started to gain speed. Reliance company started its journey on the victorious pathway!

Although Ambani was excited by the progress, he was eager for the next stage. He started to search for ways to reach the next stage!

❏❏❏

Chapter 4

'Be satisfied with what you have achieved already' is surely not for those who are in the trade. It is even dangerous for tradesmen to be satisfied with what they have achieved!

The reason is that there is no limitation for trade – the limit lies only in the minds of those who are involved in it!

If a successful petty shop owner is satisfied with his growth, he has to stay as a petty shop owner for the rest of his life. Only if he has the yearning to achieve more, he will think about expanding his petty shop into a grocery shop and work toward it. There are several opportunities in this field, a grocery shop can be developed into a supermarket and a wholesale trade. But aspiration is required to think about the opportunities. Skill alone is not enough; one should have the courage to dream big – only then success rain will pour upon you!

On observing Dhirubhai Ambani's life story, we can see several examples for this. He was never satisfied with what he had at any stage of his life. He was not overwhelmed by his success and was constantly thinking about "what next?" This quality in him enabled him to plunge into new ventures, grab the opportunities available within it and move on to the next stage!

While he was reaping good profits in the export business, Ambani was thinking about what to do next, which opportunities are favorable for his business and how to utilize them.

He had a small idea, it cannot be considered, it was just a doubt or a question he asked himself – we are exporting several things to other countries. What if we import the good items available in other countries and sell them here?

This small spark became the root cause of Ambani's wealth for the next several years and was the backbone behind Reliance's continuous growth and achievements!

No words can describe the passion Indians have for foreign goods for decades. Although they do not have food to feed them, we can look at people bragging about their imported Chinese pen or England perfume. Imported goods has always mesmerize Indians!

Ambani's instinct told him to import foreign things, especially foreign clothing brands and sell them in India to get huge profits. He started to analyze the possibilities of his idea.

Reliance had a favorable point in the Indian government's export-import policy then. That regulation said that those who wish to import anything from foreign countries, have to export something of the same value to other countries. The Government made this rule mandatory to control people from importing foreign goods without any limits. Since Reliance was already involved in exporting, their imports became easy!

Ambani decided to import an artificial fiber called Rayon. But, to do that, he was supposed to export huge quantities of spices to foreign countries. Although it was a loss, he did it and sold the imported Rayon with a wide profit margin in India, earning huge profits!

Ambani learned that Nylon had a huge demand in India. Since Rayon manufacture had started in India, he exported Rayon to the needed nations and imported Nylon instead. Ambani earned huge profits in that project too!

Remember that what Ambani considered a profit was not small gains. According to him, 'profit' meant three times on the least and seven times at the max!

Reliance grew step by step with cotton clothes, synthetic fibers, Rayon, Nylon and its next milestone was polyester!

Since Ambani decided to pursue his life in the textile field, he started learning deeply about the textile and apparel world. He analyzed everything including the advancements in the field worldwide, latest fabrics, the differences between them, its plus and minuses, which might be durable over time, which might be easily destroyable, which might suit India and which might not, which will last longer and which will tear easily. He chose Polyester after all his analysis!

There were several reasons behind Ambani's decision to choose to invest in Polyester to pave way for a successful Reliance – the major reason was the Indian market and its people!

During the mid-fifties, even before Ambani returned from Yeden, Polyester was introduced in India. Despite that, it was a slowly growing industry. Although many were involved in the Polyester trade, none can be said to reaped huge profits.

But, Ambani believed that Polyester's demand in the Indian markets will grow soon. Because Ambani predicted that Indians will be attracted by Polyester's easy to use and easy to maintain property. When compared to cotton, Polyester's properties would be appealing to the Indians.

Ambani trusted his instincts and as usual, started to trade Polyester using a huge investment. His instinct paid well, Reliance started with importing/exporting Polyester initially. Then moved on to manufacturing Polyester locally and exporting it. Slowly, Polyester occupied more than seventy percent of the Indian textile market. Although Ambani entered the Polyester industry late, only he earned huge profits and fame for the first time!

Starting from that day, till now, Polyester forms the backbone of the Reliance company. Reliance is one of the world's biggest Polyester industries to date. More gates opened to Reliance while looking out to manufacture the raw materials needed for Polyester. In short, just like Reliance's current CEO Mukesh Ambani has said 'Polyester forms the foundation of this company!'

Let us look at the name and fame Ambani got due to Polyester later. Let us move on to the new office of Reliance now!

Ambani had his tiny office in the crowded area of Mumbai named Masjid Bunder. When his business improved, he felt that moving to a better place will be beneficial. So, Reliance moved to Dhobi Talao. Ambani stepped into the brokerage business for artificial fibers from that office.

In 1965, Reliance faced a minor disturbance. The misunderstanding between the shareholders Dhirubhai Ambani and Chambaklal Damani created a few big changes in it.

Although they did trade together, there was a huge difference between the approaches of Ambani and Damani. Ambani was a bold person. If he decides to try a new venture, he will never hesitate to take risks – hope you remember him swimming among the sharks in Yeden to have an ice cream!

But, Damani was risk-averse. He hesitated to spend money in any new venture. He thought, "Isn't it enough to utilize the money that we have and continue the existing business properly? Why should we bring in unwanted trouble?". How can Ambani continue to work with somebody like him?

The crack which they had earlier, widened into a huge gap due to a decision made by Ambani in 1965. Ambani decided to start a spinning mill for Reliance. Damani did not like it. He argued "Why should we get involved in something new and burn our fingers?"

Ambani was not following Damani's fears. He believed that instead of buying and selling clothes if they weave their clothes and sell them, then the profit would be higher. He was not content in being just a trader in the business. He wanted to become a clothing manufacturer, stamping his identity and grow into a game-changer in the market – that was Ambani.

Due to this difference, Damani relieved himself from Reliance. Ambani gave him his share of the company and started the process to establish a new spinning mill.

Ambani's first spinning mill was established in his native state Gujarat at a place named Naroda which was around twenty kilometers away from Ahmedabad during the beginning of 1966. Ambani started his spinning mill with four spinning machines exported from foreign countries at the capital of two lakhs and eighty thousand rupees!

Almost during the same period, Aditya Birla, another leading business person of India purchased a company named 'Indian Rayon' and was turning it into his spinning mill. It was said that he bought Indian Rayon for thirty lakh rupees. But, Ambani built a new spinning mill for himself at a cost that was lesser by ten percent!

Since the clothing manufactured at the Naroda mill was of premium quality, Ambani exported them under the name "Reliance Textiles" to several foreign nations. With the profit earned through his exports, he repaid the loan he got for building the spinning mill within a couple of years!

As the clothing orders increased for 'Reliance Textiles', new pieces of machinery were added to the Naroda mill. Many employees were hired, the mill grew and promoted Ambani from a successful textile trader into a successful businessman!

In 1968, Ambani's family shifted from its ten-year residence 'Venilal Estates' to a bigger and better house. Ambani, who traveled only through public bus for all his business journeys, bought his first Fiat car only then.

Ambani's 'Reliance' group turned its focus from export trade into local trade. Ambani observed that Polyester clothes were gaining popularity in India during the seventies. So, he decided to sell Reliance's clothes all over India in the 1970s.

Ambani had to expand his Naroda mills several folds to achieve his target. He never hesitated to spend for a fair business need and hence, Ambani spent several lakhs in expanding his spinning mill. Ambani explored all the new techniques and good processes in textile manufacturing all over the world and implemented everything in his Naroda mill. His mission was to manufacture clothes which do not have any faults in them and to build trust among his customers that Reliance's products will always be of good quality.

Ambani's usual technique that while manufacturing in bulk quantities the price will automatically drop was applied to the Polyester clothing manufacture too. Since the clothing varieties were manufactured in a world-class factory, Reliance's polyester clothing had an extra shine than the others.

Hence, Ambani was able to produce good quality Polyester clothes at lower costs – Indian customers wanted just the same! They purchased Reliance's clothes happily and this in turn, increased the Polyester demand in India. Just like we learned earlier, seventy percent of the clothes sold in India were Polyester clothes – the major reason for that was Reliance's quality products!

In 1975, a technical team from the World Bank visited India. They wanted to visit the textile manufacturing units of our country and inspect their quality. The team traveled all over India, visited major factories in person and reported their comments to the World Bank.

They have praised the Reliance group to the sky in their reports. Their mention that 'The only Indian spinning mill which is on the same quality as those in developed nations – Reliance spinning mill in Naroda' took Reliance's name to the world.

In 1977, Reliance received another accolade which overrode World Bank's report. A Japanese reporter from 'Japan Textiles News' visited the Naroda spinning mill and wrote that such an efficient spinning mill cannot be seen even in developed countries like Japan!

While Ambani's dreams were starting to come true, he started to dream even bigger dreams. He wanted to modernize and expand his spinning mill which was already successfully running. He wanted to start other businesses related to textile manufacturing. But what about the capital for those businesses?

In that period, most Indian companies got loans from banks and other financial institutions for their business investments. But, the problem with that was that a huge part of the profit got had to be paid as interest.

Ambani did not like that. He thought, "It is my dream and my efforts, why should I share it with some third party?"

Moreover, his brain which always worked overtime formulated many new plans. No bank can equalize his speed of dreams and plans. Although it was a loan, who will provide with money when spontaneously asked for?

Ambani analyzed the pros and cons and decided that bank loans will not suit him. He had to think about some other option.

Ambani thought about it day and night and found a light – It was the plan which was sleeping inside him since 1970. He believed that if he implements the plan then, he can collect more money and many more will also profit!

His plan bloomed as a revolution in India. It solved the economic crisis of several-middle-class families and changed their lifestyles altogether!

❑❑❑

Chapter 5

In the last decade, the 'Stock market' has seen a significant rise and fall in our country. Many have dumped all their savings into it aspiring for heavy returns. Many have run back from it with whatever they got after the Harshad Mehta scandal!

Although our stock market is wobbling due to a few scandals, it is not broken. Some people allot a portion of their annual savings to purchase shares from a reputed company. Middle-class people believe that benefits are good if a developing field is identified and investing in an excellent company in that field.

The foundation of their trust is the golden age of the Indian stock market which bloomed in the late seventies. The first step into the stock market was taken by our Polyester king, Dhirubhai Ambani!

In those days, businessmen who needed money went behind financial companies which provided a loan. But, Ambani had a unique idea – instead of getting a loan from a big shot and paying them loads of interest, what if we get the amount from small investors? Their portion of profits obtained can be paid to them and it will benefit all the parties involved!

Who are small investors? They are nobody but you and me!

Instead of getting a loan of two crores from a single person, if ten rupees are obtained from twenty lakh people, it amounts to two crores in total. Business can be done with that money and consider we get a profit of forty lakh rupees from it. It can be divided among the twenty -lakh people and can be given two rupees each!

The beautiful part of this plan is that all the parties involved in it will benefit from it. For Ambani, the investment needed for his new venture is obtained easily. The ten rupees given by the public is increased to twelve rupees in a few months which benefits the public. When Reliance continues to grow and earns more profits, the twelve rupees might increase to fifteen, twenty, hundreds, or even thousands in the upcoming months!

It is not that Ambani introduced the share market in India. Although several companies have already released their shares here even before Ambani, Ambani was the first one who took it to the majority public and who utilized all the possibilities of the share market to their full extent. Hence, economists call him the 'Pioneer of the Indian share market'.

Until 1977, the Indian share market was occupied only by affluent people who knew about it. Since there was nobody to explain to the middle-class people about what is share market, how to invest in it, what are its benefits or risks, they invested in gold and real estate as usual!

Ambani observed those middle-class people. He was able to recognize a huge opportunity, a gold mine that other companies involved in the share market failed to spot!

Middle-class people might not have huge savings, but they are huge in number. Ambani's business brain calculated that if those who are everywhere in India invest their savings in the share market, a huge amount can be collected and new business ventures can be tried.

But, how to make them invest in the share market? This was the question that he had then?

Since Ambani was from a modest family background, he understood the worries and fear of the common people. Not only share market, they think twice before investing in any new venture. They expect a guarantee that their money will not be lost. Because they have toiled hard for each paisa of their investment and they will never want to lose it!

Hence, trust has to be built among them that investing in the share market is good for their future and the invested money will not go away or get lost. Ambani believed that once that trust is built, the rest will happen on its own.

Based on this psychological fact, advertisements were prepared for Reliance shares. As a first step, Ambani named the shares of his company as 'Reliance Khazana' – which means Reliance treasure! He made sure to create a first impression on the public that it was a golden investment.

Ambani, who entered the share market with heavy preparation was clear on his objective – Our country's simple people are the ones who will collect the investment needed for Reliance's future, I will do all I can for their benefit!

Reliance's shares were announced in November 1977 – Ambani announced to release twenty-eight lakh shares at the rate of ten rupees each. When they reached the market in January 1978, their value has raised to 23 rupees. The welcome that Reliance's shares got among the public can be understood through this!

Ambani made another arrangement to take Reliance's shares to the next stage. His people went to the residential areas of middle-class people, explained and marketed about share market, Reliance and the benefits of investing in Reliance. They filled the application forms for those who expressed interest in it!

There were a few who could not bear Ambani's growth and they preached not to buy Reliance's shares. Ambani's business opponents tried to brainwash people saying

'Reliance is good for nothing company similar to a soap bubble. Do not trust it. Buy international companies' shares like Colgate, Levers and others. Only they can be trusted to be available for a longer duration' But investors ignored their claims.

Within a few days, Reliance's shares were wondered upon all over the nation. The majority of the public did not even know about the basics of the share market. But they knew that Reliance was a reliable textile company. They wanted to buy the company's shares based on their trust in the company's products.

Government employees, farmers, small merchants, retired/senior citizens enquired and gathered information about Reliance investments. Almost sixty thousand people bought Reliance shares and Reliance company got 2.8 crores of rupees from them!

Although it was Ambani's idea, he did not expect such a welcome from the public. He was moved by the interest shown by Indians in investing in Reliance. His desire to do something for them grew another step then. Ambani mentioned that 'each of you who has trusted us and invested your hard-earned money in our company is a member of our Reliance family'. Since then whenever he talked about his investors, he mentioned them as 'Reliance family'!

Reliance utilized the amount collected through selling its shares in 1977 in expanding its Naroda mill and other new ventures. Since then, it has become a ritual for Reliance to release its shares for each of its new projects and people buying them with interest!

There was an emotional bond between Ambani and Reliance's shareholders. He made several comforts for them which were never imagined by other companies. Each of the company's growth and announcements were sent in the post to all the thousands and later lakhs of investors. Reliance kept them informed about the status of their amount, how much they had earned and when will they receive the total amount periodically through letters.

It was said that the letters sent by Reliance to its shareholders increased several times and the postal department was overwhelmed by it. So, Ambani sent a place's letters to the Reliance employees who went to that particular place for official reasons and asked them to post the letters there!

Is it enough to just receive letters for the amount they invested in? What was the benefit received by those who trusted Reliance and invested their hard-earned money? That is a huge success story!

Since Reliance continued to run successfully, the amount invested by its shareholders also grew healthily. Consider you have bought a Reliance share at the rate of ten rupees. The value of that share is twenty rupees today and it will increase to thirty rupees in the next three months. Within a few more months it will be amplified to forty rupees. Whenever you have a money need, you can sell the share that you have and get the money needed.

This was the regular activity done by all the companies. But they could not manage to grow exponentially like

Reliance. Moreover, Ambani shared a part of Reliance's profits as dividends or as a bonus amount, or as extra shares to those who have invested in Reliance. There is no need to explain how beneficial those 'sudden' bonuses were to middle-class people!

Other companies used to make sure that the value of their shares does not cross a certain limit. But, Ambani acted against it. Reliance shares value continued to increase and never faced a huge downfall. The main reason for that was Ambani's careful and vigilant activities.

Ambani considered his shareholders' benefit in whatever decision he had to take related to Reliance. Ambani's close friends and officers say that if he comes to know that a certain decision might affect his shareholders, he will try his best to avoid making such a decision!

For example, when the Indian government decided to impose a double tax on the dividend earned through the share market, Reliance would not be affected by it. But, Ambani realized that his shareholders will be highly affected by this move and talked to his political friends to strongly voice his opposition in the Parliament. He has worked for the benefit of those who have invested in him on several occasions!

When the public understood that they enjoy several benefits by investing in Reliance, they started to buy Reliance shares with more awareness. Reliance shareholders count increased slowly from sixty thousand and reached several lakhs. If somebody slips in the share market, he would fall over a Reliance shareholder. Reliance obtained public support to such an extent.

Although Ambani was pleased by the demand for Reliance's shares among the public, there were a few funny incidents too.

Any company which runs its business by accepting money from the public has to gather its investors at a particular place once a year and declare its profit-loss details. It was an annual meeting that was established for the benefit of the investors.

In general, these meetings were held at a hotel inside a closed room. But, how to accommodate the lakhs of investors belonging to the 'Reliance family' inside a hotel?

Hence, Reliance's annual meetings were held in huge playgrounds. The places were arranged, thousands of chairs were rented, food parcels were given to the huge groups of shareholders and in short, Reliance's annual meetings were nothing short of a political conference.

More than a political conference, it can be compared to a royal 'Durbar'. Dhirubhai Ambani used to speak in front of thousands of shareholders like a monarch. Whenever he mentioned Reliance in his speech, he made sure that he used the word 'your company'. The shareholders felt more connected to him when they heard his words!

Most of the businessmen use these annual meetings to show a few undecipherable charts and to brag about their own company. But, Ambani had a different goal – the majority of the people who had invested in his company did not know anything about the stock market. They believed that investing in Reliance was better than investing it in banks and gave their entire savings. Ambani believed that it was his duty to make those people understand, to give them confidence and to improve their share market knowledge.

Most of Reliance's investors were from Gujarat. Hence, Ambani used to converse in Gujarati too in those annual meetings. He insisted not to trust his words alone and to see the growth of their investment by themselves. He advised them to read newspapers about business news, to know about Reliance through those newspapers and to compare their understanding with them!

Ambani did not want to exploit his investors' ignorance and wanted to bring them to his height as they were a part of the Reliance family.

***

Reliance as a company earned a trustable name and satisfied customers as its immovable assets both inside and outside the country. It continued to earn profits. So, Reliance's value too increased according to its growth. The growth was not an ordinary one – it was a gigantic growth that could reach the sky!

A small example can be quoted here to make you understand the enormity of the profits the investors got due to the Reliance shares at that time.

Consider a person who purchased hundred Reliance shares for thousand rupees in 1977 when the Reliance shares were introduced. He placed his shares certificate in a safe and neither took it out nor sold it for twenty-five years.

In the year 2002, he will be having 512 shares including his initial shares and the bonus shares which were given over the years. According to 2002's market, the value of those 512 shares was one lakh and forty thousand!

Moreover, he would have got more than twenty-five thousand rupees in those twenty-five years as dividends. So, the thousand rupees invested in 1977 valued one lakh and sixty-five thousand rupees in 2002. The amount he invested in Reliance has grown more than 165 times in twenty-five years!

Just think about it, can we expect such a growth in a post office or banks or even in private financial institutions which gives half a sovereign gold for a lakh of deposit?

The public opted for Reliance shares for this reason. Applications to buy Reliance shares were sold on platforms. In the latter days, when Ambani decided to step into the petroleum trade, the public rushed to buy 'Reliance Petroleum' shares even though people in general frown upon the oil industry!

Reliance's shares were respected as a social status in the society. People who held Reliance shares were looked up high with respect. Many sold their Reliance shares and married off their daughters or sent their sons to study abroad! It is also said that Reliance shares certificates were given as dowry in a few marriages that were held in North India!

Even today, if you ask anybody who holds Reliance shares, they will have an emotional story behind it. A small amount that was invested long back would have amplified and would have helped them unexpectedly. Reliance was a turning point for many Indian families.

Not only for individuals, but Reliance's arrival is also looked upon as a boon for the Indian share market. The share market was regularized only after Reliance's entry. Ambani's Reliance was the first company that understood the needs of its investors and provided them their needs. Since other companies were expected to do the same, the Indian share market improved.

In short, it can be said that without Ambani the Indian share market would not have grown to its present state!

***

Reliance's influence is still there in the share market. Reliance's shareholders' count is around fifty lakhs now; it is one of the biggest shareholders' groups in the world!

The group which preached against purchasing Reliance shares is seen nowhere now. But, Ambani did not forget about their false preaching. It is said that he used to make fun of himself as a burst soap bubble to his friends!

In 1999, Business Barons magazine awarded Dhirubhai Ambani the 'Twentieth century's Best Indian businessman' award. When Ambani received the awards, he spoke about his loyal shareholders who have invested in his company.

"I think about what I did in all these years. My company and I are one of the reasons for the prosperity and happiness in fifty lakh families. We made those family members be well and happy and that gives me an immense satisfaction",

Ambani said. He also expressed his huge desire, "But, I cannot consider it done and retire. We have to continue doing what we did so far. We have to expand and do it bigger. If we were able to do it for fifty lakh families, couldn't we do it bigger for fifty crore families? Shouldn't we do it?"

Chapter 6

Once Reliance's entry into the share market was successfully completed in 1977-78, the next issue which bothered Ambani was the few problems he had in sending Reliance's textile products to all the parts of India.

Reliance depended on a few bulk sellers and agents to distribute and sell its textile products which were produced in Naroda of Gujarat district to other parts of India. But these sellers showed great interest in selling huge companies' products and not to the products of a developing company like Reliance!

Due to their negligence, complaints arose that the Reliance products were not available properly in several areas. Ambani investigated the root cause of such complaints and took immediate action!

The problem happened due to the textile agents who wanted the entire textile market under their control. What if we forego those agents and open shops under the Reliance's direct management all over the country? What if we send the products directly to the store and support them?

The plan sounded profitable. But there were lots of issues in implementing such a plan. Small-scale merchants had to be found who were willing to sell the Reliance's products. After finding them, all the arrangements to open a textile shop have to be made. The products they want to sell have to be sent properly, the accounts have to be monitored each month, payments for the sold goods have to be collected and returns have to be made for unsold goods. Amidst everything the sellers have to be monitored if they are reliable or if they might abscond – in short, it was a huge headache!

But, if everything is done properly, profit will be more than the efforts spent. Since there will be no agents in between, Reliance will get more profit from sales. At the same time, the sellers also will get more profits. Since the sellers will be under their direct management, they can fix the products and advertisements based on their individual needs!

Ambani analyzed each of the above points and waved his green signal for the project. Since the project promised benefit for both the Reliance the sellers, Ambani expected it to be a huge hit just like his share market success.

His expectation proved to be real. Reliance direct stores were opened all over the country and they had a huge welcome. Reliance bagged another huge victory among the others who wanted to crush it!

In 1978, Ambani wanted to give a brand name for Reliance's textile products. The name has to be simple so that it embeds in a common man's heart. Only then the name will be memorable for them. And when they want to purchase clothes, they can ask the salesperson for the particular brand.

After long consideration, Ambani chose the name Vimal. It was the name of Ambani's elder brother Ramnik Bhai's eldest son.

Once he chose the brand name 'Vimal', Ambani decided to make it a common name that each Indian utters. He wanted to make sure that 'Vimal' is better than all the other clothing brands. What is the way to achieve that? Advertisements!

Therefore, advertisements for Vimal started to crowd in print media, TV and everywhere else. 'Vimal sarees' and 'Vimal clothing' were the talk of the town!

Among these continuous advertisements, 'Vimal sarees' advertisements were the ones that popularized the 'Vimal' brand name. The advertisement was enjoyed by all the Indians and it said: A woman expresses herself in many languages. One among them is Vimal!

After that the slogan 'Only Vimal' was introduced. The single statement spread the brand 'Vimal' to each corner of India and raised it to the peak of the Indian textile market!

Since then, 'Vimal' has become the identity of Reliance company. In the 'Most trusted and wanted Indian brand' selection conducted by 'Economic Times' in 2002, Vimal got the first place in the clothing section!

Reliance manufactured and sold varieties of clothing under the name 'Vimal'. Most of them were polyester clothes. The reason was that India was under a Polyester spell at that time and Reliance utilized the demand wisely.

But, Ambani felt that there was a small loophole in it. He felt that importing the raw materials needed for the manufacture of polyester products from the foreign countries was cost consuming. He wanted to produce them in India!

Apart from the monetary benefits the plan held, there were several other major advantages to the plan. First was that we need not depend on anybody for manufacturing our textiles. What if the country that sends the raw materials to us decides not to send them anymore? What if they send low-quality raw materials which might affect the quality of our finished goods? If we produce them ourselves, we need not bother about these questions. Moreover, if we manufacture the raw materials ourselves, we can sell them to other Polyester companies in India and export them to other countries. That will be an added business too!

Ambani's this plan was the first step in fulfilling one of his long-term desire. His dream project can be said as 'backward integration'!

Let us learn about backward integration now itself as we will look at this technique several times in Ambani's history.

We will be astonished at how much he had achieved using a single formula!

Backward integration - The name might be threatening, but it is a common technique that requires a wider vision and confidence!

Consider you own a tea shop. You buy the tea powder and coffee powder which you use daily from Kuppusamy and co. The milk comes from the Gopalasamy depot. You use the powder and milk and make tea and coffee. You get a profit of hundred rupees a day.

Now, you get an idea – Gopalasamy increases the milk's rate now and then. Moreover, his milk is also too watery. What if you buy a cow and produce your milk instead of depending on that cheating fellow?

That is a genuine plan. You buy a new cow using the savings you have or by getting a loan from the bank. You take care of the cow, milk it regularly and utilize the milk it gives. Although the expense is a bit higher in this, you get a profit of a hundred and fifty per day instead of a hundred per day!

What you did here is backward integration – Instead of buying milk, you milk your cow. Due to this, your basic business tea shop gets more profit. After a few days, if you develop an interest in your new business (raising a cow and milking it!), you can buy another cow, milk it and sell the excess milk to other tea shops or houses! It will fetch you more profit!

Another example of backward integration plan which is similar to the one mentioned above. The price of Kuppusamy & co.'s tea powder is high. What if we buy a tea estate and grow our tea leaves?

Do not get shocked at the prospect of a tea shop owner buying a tea estate. Just like we read before, backward integration requires confidence and an independent mind which prefers to come out of the usual limitations to aim for the peak!

Producing all the raw materials needed for our basic business and not depending upon anybody for anything. Selling the raw materials which we produce (example: milk, tea powder) to other merchants and earn a profit! This is backward integration is short!

Ambani did the same on a larger scale. He started with selling clothing and entered into producing clothes. After that, he started to produce the raw materials needed. A few chemicals were needed to produce the raw materials. So, he started manufacturing them. Since the chemicals were obtained from Petroleum, he entered into the petroleum sector too. He went back at each step and at one point, he reached a complacency where Reliance manufactured everything from the basic raw materials to the completed product!

We will look at everything in detail. Now, let us return to the Polyester problem.

Naroda mill which started in 1966 with a capital of lesser than three lakhs, was producing in crores during the eighties. Ambani wanted to develop it further through his first annexure of producing raw materials for Polyester!

The major raw materials needed for the production of Polyester were Polyester Staple Fiber (PSF) and Polyester Filament Yarn (PFY). Reliance decided to manufacture both in India. Several locations were evaluated and finally, a place named Patalganga which was about 65 kilometers away from Mumbai was chosen as the right place.

During that time, Ambani received helping hands from his elder son Mukesh Ambani. Mukesh Ambani was a chemical engineer who has completed his MBA from the US Stanford University. Dhirubhai decided that his chemical knowledge and management skills will help the Patalganga factory. Mukesh Ambani joined Reliance in 1981 and was involved completely in the construction of the Patalganga factory.

Following him, Dhirubhai Ambani's youngest son Anil Ambani joined Reliance in 1983. He too majored in Chemistry and did his MBA at the Wharton University.

Dhirubhai Ambani's two sons shared his dreams and worked hard toward them. These two brothers' contributions played a major role in Reliance's growth for the next twenty years!

In 1982, a factory was installed in Patalganga to manufacture PFY. Twenty-five year old Mukesh Ambani held the complete responsibility of that factory. He took it as a challenge and completed the construction work of the factory within one and a half year which normally would have taken two years to complete. This industry which spreads over three hundred acres of land and running at world-class quality is one of Reliance's proudest achievements.

Following that, a sector to manufacture PSF in Patalganga in 1986. Ambani found all the latest and efficient techniques available all over the world in the manufacturing field and implemented everything in his factory. The manufactured products from this factory were of the topmost quality. Patalganga industries manufactured around ten thousand tons of raw materials each year. This completed Reliance's polyester manufacturing process and profit were also earned by selling those raw materials to other traders in the same field!

The next step in Reliance's backward integration plan was to manufacture Purified Terephthalic Acid (PTA) which was the raw material needed to manufacture PSF and PFY which was already being produced in the Patalganga factories. Following that was the manufacture of Paraxylene which was the raw material of PTA and it went on. In short, if they could manufacture everything that is needed to produce Polyester in Patalganga, there will be no need to depend on anybody for anything.

PTA manufacturing sector was started in Patalganga in 1986. Within the next two years, all the materials needed for the production of Paraxylene and PTA were manufactured there internally. Apart from these, from 1987, Reliance started to produce Linear Alkyl Benzene (LAB) which was used in the manufacturing process of detergent powder in the Patalganga facility and sold it.

Within 1988, Reliance became one of the major chemical producers of India through its Patalganga industries. Companies that were considered rivals to Reliance were forced to purchase the raw materials needed from Reliance. Reliance's pennant flew higher than all others!

But, despite its growth Reliance did not ignore its first and basic business—clothing manufacture. Ambani was clear that all other businesses should run on the strong foundation – the textile business. Hence, Reliance utilized the chemicals produced in Patalganga and multiplied its polyester production. 'Vimal' took an unwavering place amidst Indians' hearts and hence sales were also high. Reliance faced profit and growth on all fronts!

Not only Reliance, but also our country faced many benefits through it. Since Reliance manufactured and sold several chemicals which were imported from foreign countries so far, imports to India were reduced. This paved a way for India to achieve self-sufficiency in textile manufacture.

Moreover, since the chemicals produced in India were cheaper and had more quality than those which were imported, it benefited the overall industrial development!

We should think about the factors which enabled a mere clothing seller named Ambani to succeed in such a massive project. Ambani's success was not bagged in a single day or a single week or a single month. It was a dream which was cultured over several years by analyzing everything, thinking about the possibilities, calculating the risks and planning to ease those risks!

Ambani's friends mentioned that he had a 'secret' paper kept inside his pocket since the day he started his business. The paper had a map in it. It had 'textiles' at its bottom, above it was the raw materials needed for textile manufacture, above it was the 'grandfather' materials needed to manufacture those raw materials and above it was the 'great grandfather' materials needed. The tree grew step by step and above everything was the greatest of all the grandfathers, 'petroleum' which mines crude petroleum and purifies it!

That was his long-term plan. Starting from mining crude petroleum from the soil to the production of clothing and selling them, Reliance was involved in everything from the start to the end! It had an influence in everything and it ruled as a monarch in the business world. That was his desire, wish, aspiration and everything!

A few minutes and a creative mind are enough to dream. But, courage, faith, confidence and untiring hard work are required to make those dreams come true. Ambani had everything that was needed to bring his dreams to reality. All those who worked under him understood his dreams. They contributed their part in achieving his dreams. With their help, Ambani turned his dreams into reality in twenty years!

Reliance took its first and firm step in the petroleum industry which was at the top of its backward integration chain during the beginning of the nineties. We have to look at a major problem before we go into the petroleum sector – A few bad accusations and their effects which affected Ambani's personal and public life!

How did Ambani and Reliance came out of that blazing fire of charges is an interesting story filled with excitement, thrill, tragedy and determination!

Chapter 7

Just like there is some darkness beneath the bright flame of a candle, a few dark pages in every successful person's history are real. But only time can answer the question if those pages are dark or if the disgruntled people who were jealous of his growth have covered them with a screen!

When a single person without any prior experience and guidance entered the industrial world with less than a lakh as his capital amount, reached great heights, there is no wonder that a few murmurs erupted.

Some were jealous, some were angry, some were bitter and some were just curious. Due to various reasons like the ones mentioned before, several stories were speculated about Ambani in the media. There were a few magazines that wrote that Ambani's entire growth was through illegal route and they picturized him as a fraud!

At a stage, it was said that Ambani got so irritated by a stream of incessant notorious news about him that he decided never to talk to any media person. He did not give an interview to any media representative and did not answer any allegation that was made against him. At the same time, all the Reliance companies were running successfully as ever. Their shares continued to skyrocket and people continued to benefit from them!

We have to understand something before we look in detail into the various arraignments blamed upon Ambani and his justifications for that starting from the sixties – running a business in India is not just about producing a commodity and selling it. There are numerous steps for running a business, there are strict government rules which control exports, imports and local market, and then there are government officials. Even if an entrepreneur does not like it, all the above together constitute the Indian business world!

Even a small petty shop owner who runs his shop by the corner has to meet a few officers, submit his application and run his business only after getting their approval. In such a situation, it becomes a necessity for the people who run huge industries to comply with the government.

Such entrepreneurs being close with a few government officers and requesting them to decide based upon their preferences is not a strange happening in our country. They have to spend a fortune on that and this is also common here!

All the troubles have to be endured because the government is a giant machine. Just like a machine that runs on diesel, the government is a huge machine that runs on regulations and laws. It does not understand the problems of a common man. It insists everything to run according to the rules. Nobody can deny that.

But it does not understand the practicality that the person standing before it has spent lakhs and crores, if a particular consent takes four days to get released it might cause a loss of several thousand. It runs according to the rules. There is no way to include such 'humane' things into a machine's instructions.

Due to these reasons, entrepreneurs of those days maintained a smooth relationship with the officers who ran the government machine. Files were approved and orders were given at the right time due to their 'kindness'.

In a situation where such 'diplomacies' were considered a part of Indian business, Ambani stepped into the business world. Without any prior experience, he knocked on every door and wall of Delhi's government buildings for each of his business approvals.

Sociologists mention the period when Ambani started export trade as the era of 'License Raj'. It meant 'License Empire'. You cannot start any business just because you have money with you. For whatever trade you wish to indulge in, a license has to be obtained. Even if you want to collect the twigs from your backyard and sell them, you need a license!

The government does not provide you the license easily. They analyze everything ranging from how many from your neighborhood are planning to do the same business like you, who might be affected when you are given the approval, who will be benefited, who else from India has applied to sell their twigs like you, how many percentages of them are approved in each state when compared to that value have the number of licenses allotted to your state has been given and so on.

In short, getting a license depends upon the Almighty or upon the mighty people who rule us!

In such a period when there were thousands of conditions and several strict regulations, almost all of the Indian entrepreneurs were terrified of the License empire. Although they were able to obtain licenses as per their needs through off-screen methods, nobody dared to fight against those strict regulations directly!

Economic researchers mention that Ambani must be the first entrepreneur who read and understood the complex regulations and ambiguous laws of the License Empire and utilized it for the benefit of his own company. But he did not step out of law at any time. If he had done that, he would not have been able to continue his business.

Ambani's intelligence and his skill to find out opportunities amidst chaos raised him as a successful entrepreneur overcoming the regulations of License Empire.

Ambani proved that the government regulations which everybody considered as a block can be transformed into a stepping stone by climbing upon them.

He considered the government and its regulations as a part of his business. Consider a stubborn person and we have to get something from him. Should we fight with him or should we tactically deal with him by going along his way and complete our mission? Isn't it a knack to achieve what we want through subtlety?

Ambani's tact was looked upon as a huge crime by his opponents. They started to criticize his ways as illegal instead of learning from his novel approach. They preached that Ambani was connected to higher government officers and political leaders. They said that Ambani got instant approval through his connections.

A part of their indictments was true – Ambani had several friends among the most influential people of the government. But, the answer to the question, 'if he exploited their friendship' is unproven.

For example, Pranab Mukherjee who was the Finance Minister during the then Congress rule was Ambani's close friend. He once said that Ambani's approach to face every situation as a challenge to himself attracted him and that made them close friends. He said, "He is close with several ministers like me. Some say that he used us to advance his business. But India's financial situation was so strict then. So, he had to meet several people for the sake of his business. How could you say that all those people are his cronies?"

People who have analyzed the industrial growth and fall of the Indian industries of that period will accept the truth in Pranab Mukherjee's words. Only when those who ran their business amidst severe regulations let the government and government officers know about their struggles and the severity of those regulations, the laws would be changed according to the period. If everybody stays silent, then who will bell the cat?

Ambani boldly took several actions during the period when several entrepreneurs were smothered by the license demon. He proved that there is no use in bad-mouthing about the government rules and instead the best approach is to utilize them for our benefit.

For example, as we have seen before, the government's law was to export something to import something. Ambani's astute approach to that regulation was to export under loss and to balance that loss while selling the imported goods – the loss he endured in exporting spices was more than balanced when he sold the imported Rayon at three times profit! In this way, he did not violate any government rules and at the same time, he has earned a considerable profit!

Ambani's such actions invited huge criticism. His competitors started to spread the news that Ambani has cheated the government and he has bent the government rules according to his needs with the help of the rulers.

Just like any other merchant, Ambani too wanted his company to yield considerable profit. But he had certain general goals too. It is said that whenever he discussed with the officials, he has argued in favor of everybody considering him as a representative of the Indian industrial world.

For example, people quote the incident when Ambani tried to reduce the tax imposed on importing some artificial fibers. Those fibers were an important raw material for his business. He would indeed have earned maximum profit by reducing the tax on the fibers. But, at the same time, by reducing the import tax, textile smuggling which was common during that period has reduced a lot!

Likewise, the Indian government which had a severe policy that only the government agencies can involve in oil purifying relaxed and decided to allow private companies into the field. Several media quoted that Ambani, with his relentless efforts, was the major reason for this change. There were also accusations that Reliance wanted to enter into oil purifying business and that prompted Ambani to change the government regulations.

But, in truth, it is beneficial to the Indian economy when private parties also enter into such huge businesses. The domination by government agencies was changed, healthy competition was ensured, the quality of the end products was improved, the export rate was increased and in general, the nation's financial situation was improved due to the change made by the government. Now, when we look at the globalization happening in almost all the industries, we can understand the importance of Ambani's foresight!

Similarly, every action by Ambani can be looked upon as a selfish act, but, when closely observed, we can look at the benefit it has made on the public. It is similar to the popular dialog from the movie Prashakthi, "My selfish actions have public welfare imbibed in it!"

Ambani's childhood friend and current member of the Rajya Sabha, Murli Deora says, "Ambani's wish is to include entrepreneurs in creating the government policies, laws, regulations and rules related to industrial growth".

Ambani states that "Only we know about the day-to-day struggle that we face. So, only we can help the government to consider our issues while the formulation of a regulation". Ambani has discussed this with Murli Deora several times and he has also asked him to mention his comments in the Parliamentary speech during the debate on industrial growth!

***

A few of the accusations thrown upon Ambani are either astonishing or hilarious!

Everybody knew that Ambani had acquaintances belonging to almost all the parties. But it was rumored that Ambani was close with all the ministers, chief ministers, prime ministers and everybody else, hence his business would not be affected no matter who came to power!

Apart from these, there were numerous speculations that several MPs were under Ambani's control and he could make or break any government if we wanted to!

The biggest rumor among all the allegations was that Ambani was friends with all the military officers of Pakistan. One of Ambani's factories located in Jamnagar of Gujarat was located close to the Pakistan border. So, a few magazines have written hilarious articles that Ambani has made a secret deal with Pakistan that if the Indo-Pakistan war arises, his factory should be spared!

We have to note something here – Ambani socialized with everybody, he did not voluntarily make enemies and tried to be friends with everybody. He considered that people who are in trade should have a pleasing personality. It is said that he has said, "I never hesitated to gratify anybody"!

We have to mention an interesting incident as said by his son-in-law Dattaraj Salgaocar regarding this.

During the beginning of the eighties, Salgaocar has just completed his MBA in the US and returned home. He decided to continue his family business and was knocking on the doors of Delhi to procure licenses.

Young, active and American-educated Dattaraj Salgaocar was soon frustrated by the slow approach and strict policies of the Indian government. He got vexed with the government offices and their shuttling nature.

During that situation, he met Ambani on a Delhi-Mumbai flight. Since Dattaraj's father and Ambani were childhood friends, he was acquainted with Ambani's family from a young age! (Dattaraj Salgaocar loved and married Ambani's daughter Deepti later!)

Ambani just politely asked about Dattaraj's well-being. Dattaraj Salgaocar started to vent about all his problems as if he was waiting for Ambani's inquiry. The content of his vent was this: Why are the government's regulations so confusing and complex? I have the capital amount and I use it to start a business. Why don't they just allow that to happen? Why should I beg so many times to start a business with my own money?

Ambani listened to Dattaraj's outburst patiently and then said, "Imagine, you are planning to conduct a puja at your house. You have to sit before the deity for hours, offer flowers and other holy things and perform a lot of things, am I right?"

Dattaraj did not understand where Ambani was going with that line of logic and just nodded his head.

"The puja gets completed at last. Would you be able to have your food immediately after that? No! You have to pay the priest who conducted the puja, you have to feed him, you have to feed the guests, cows, crows and others. Only after completing everything, you can have your food, am I right?"

Dattaraj nodded again.

"When you eat your food after completing your work, your food will be tastier than before. Have you realized it?", asked Ambani. "The Indian industries and government are similar to that. You can enjoy your rights only after satisfying many. But, remember that after completing all the tasks, your food will be tastier. So, be patient and do not lose hope", he advised Dattaraj.

***

There were several accusations like Ambani held the government under his control, he violated laws and have cheated. But, at the same time, no other company has helped in the growth of the Indian economy and Indian industry like Reliance. For example, Reliance alone manufactures five percentage of the total goods exported from India to the foreign countries!

While talking about those who accuse him, Ambani said, "My skin is thicker, I am used to their comments and false accusations." He preferred to concentrate on Reliance's growth than to waste his precious time in fighting against those faceless accusers.

***

But not everybody who waged war against them are faceless. A few political and industrial bigshots formed an army against Ambani and fought with him. Several plots were framed against Ambani and the media propaganda has happened to portray Ambani as a charlatan. Those rivals tried to crush Ambani and his business through any route!

Many expected Ambani to fall due to their attacks which were formulated with a heavy vengeance. Many even pitied that a full stop has been kept to Ambani's success story which had steady growth until then!

In the direct war which continued for several years, Ambani and his adversaries had severe competition. Although the enemies' hands seemed to dominate at times, Ambani won at the end of the war.

But the price he paid for his victory was huge!

❑❑❑

Chapter 8

Dhirubhai Ambani used to say that his great success was his first and foremost enemy.

There is truth in his weariness. Ambani entered the Indian industrial world during the late fifties, grew his business higher than all the experts of that time and turned his brainchild Reliance into India's leading private company, this earned him jealousy from others!

Those bigshots were wary because Ambani was a fresher in the field. He landed from Yeden one day and grew into a non-negligible force in the Indian industrial world.

But they could not do anything except talking behind Ambani's back. The reason was that Ambani dealt with his company with utmost concentration and care. His hard work evolved into continuous successes. So, Ambani and Reliance crossed each achievement and were on their way to the peak!

At the same time, Ambani earned so many enemies in his career as much success he earned. All his enemies joined force and were looking for the right opportunity to crush him.

The first attack was at the end of April 1982 in Kolkata.

Reliance company's shares were at a respectable place in the Indian share market during that period. Due to the trust people had in Reliance and Ambani who were performing extraordinarily, Reliance shareholders were at peace. According to their belief, the amount they invested in Reliance will only grow and can never diminish!

A small gang tried to dissolve that trust shareholders had. They planned to announce that Reliance has planned to sell lakhs of its shares at a very low rate. When anybody hears that announcement, they would think that Reliance is facing a severe loss and hence the sale. In that case, they also will try to sell their Reliance shares at whatever price that is offered. If everybody did the same, Reliance shares' value would decline automatically and that would give a bad reputation to Ambani and Reliance. Investors who had trusted them so far would lose their respect and abandon Ambani!

The plan was an effective one, but, when they tried to implement it, Ambani gave them a return favor which attacked them with amplified force!

Everything happened according to their plan initially. Due to the shareholders who believed that the Reliance's shares are being sold at a lower rate, Reliance share's market value dropped from Rs. 130/- to Rs. 120/-!

But, Ambani realized that his adversaries were trying to spoil his reputation at an earlier stage itself. He framed a tactical plan to counteract!

He requested the cooperation of several share market agents in Kolkata to execute his plan. They extended their support and Ambani's counteraction against the enemies started!

Ambani planned to go along with his enemy's plan and to attack them. He planned to 'buy the shares' which his enemies were planning 'to sell'!

According to it, share market dealers who favored Ambani met each of the enemy gang members who said that they were selling Reliance shares. They accepted to buy the shares at the rate mentioned and paid the said amount. If they had ten shares or lakh shares, the dealers bought everything!

Likewise, Ambani's friend dealers bought all the shares that were rumored to be sold!

The next step of the plan was for the dealers to meet the enemy gang members and demand the shares. They had paid the full amount in advance and demanded with force for the shares that were supposed to be sold!

But, how can the fraud gang give them the shares? They do not have Reliance shares in real!

The gang realized that they had fallen into their own grave. It is said that they apologized to Ambani for their mistake and paid a huge amount as a penalty. Only after that, they were able to untangle the mess they created!

Everybody believed that the problem was over when Ambani himself interfered and solved the plot planned against him. But, Ambani's enemies were not ready to leave him as such.

They questioned the source of the money which Ambani used to buy lakhs of Reliance shares. This question echoed all over the world and was discussed in Parliament.

Finance minister Pranab Mukherjee answered that question, "During 1982-83 financial year, several NRIs invested 22 crores in Reliance. Their investment was utilized during the crisis!"

Although the government put a full stop to the issue with that explanation, a few investigative journals raised questions about the NRIs who invested in Reliance. Hence, an investigation was ordered by the Reserve Bank of India to look into the issue.

The Reserve Bank of India announced at the end of the investigation that neither Ambani nor Reliance did anything illegal in that issue.

So, although it created a major stir, Dhirubhai Ambani won the final victory in the Kolkata share market war!

***

Another VIP who had friction with Dhirubhai Ambani was VP Singh – Viswanath Pratap Singh who was the finance minister in Rajeev Gandhi's cabinet and who later was India's Prime Minister!

During the initial growth of Ambani, Indira Gandhi ruled India. Ambani who had the policy of never rubbing the wrong side of the government maintained a smooth relationship with Indira Gandhi's government.

When Indira Gandhi was killed in 1984 and when her son Rajeev Gandhi became the Prime Minister of India, Ambani was worried. The reason was the new finance minister VP Singh!

As Ambani's expected, problems started in May 1985. As a first block, the government imposed several restrictions in importing PTA which was the major raw material needed for the manufacture of Polyester products. It was announced that a fifty percent tax would be imposed on PTA imports. Due to these decisions, Reliance faced additional costs and huge losses.

The trials against Reliance and Ambani continued. In 1984, several banks were indicted that they have given loans without any questions to a few financial groups started by Ambani. Reserve Banks of India investigated the issues and ordered the loan to be collected back.

Amidst everything, one of the most popular news companies, 'Indian Express' turned against Ambani. Indian Express started to publish negative news against Ambani continuously!

The news was planned perfectly and was published at regular intervals, they tried to spoil the 'good boy' image that Ambani had and portray him as a swindler. It was said that Indian Express publisher Ramnath Goenka was behind everything. What vengeance would he have against Ambani?

Ambani's business rival 'Bombay Dyeing's chairperson Nusli Wadia was Ramnath Goenka's close friend. It was said that Indian Express waged its article war against Ambani due to the trigger given by Wadia.

VP Singh's cabinet added fuel to the blaze further. When Ambani planned to produce a chemical named PFY in India and sell it locally, the government withdrew the import tax imposed upon the product. Hence, both the imported PFY and local (Ambani's produce) PFY were sold at almost the same rate. Guess what would the public prefer to buy?

Experts started to look at Ambani and Reliance with worry as they were attacked from all directions. They even suspected if Ambani's enemies' claim that Ambani developed his business with the support of the government. The reason was that Ambani started to face trouble only when Indira Gandhi's government ended all of a sudden and when Rajeev Gandhi's government started. Reliance faced its first loss only then!

But, Ambani overcame everybody's predictions and came out of the rubbish with flying colors. The first sign of his comeback was when his company's debenture worth 500 crores were released in seven editions and each time it was sold as soon as it was released. It proved that despite all the negative news and propaganda, people still trusted Ambani!

Soon, VP Singh's cabinet position was changed from Finance minister. Nusli Wadia was strongly accused under FERA (active then) law which handled foreign currency regulations. Indian Express was also accused of several irregularities and its buildings all over India were raided by the government. Based on the pieces of evidence obtained in those raids, several cases were filed on Indian Express!

So, Ambani won the final victory in that battle too – amidst all the commotions, Reliance company continued to run successfully. He had public support and on top of everything, the right action was taken on his enemies!

A black mark among his successes was a personal loss faced by Ambani. Due to the continuous physical and mental strain due to all the above crises, Ambani suffered a cardiac stroke on February 9, 1986. Half of his body was paralyzed following the stroke.

Chapter 9

Although a single person building an industrial empire is something to be proud of, there is a huge threat to it. The company and the person cannot be looked upon as different entities. When there is a small discomfort to that person, everybody related to the company will be terrified about the future of the company. It is similar to the fear many had when Tendulkar got ousted from a game!

When Ambani had a cardiac stroke in 1986, everybody who was associated with Reliance and its investors was shocked. While all of them were praying for his speedy recovery, his enemies might have celebrated it.

Ambani too was aware of the happenings around him. While he was getting treated at Mumbai's Jaslok hospital, he enquired his well-wishers if there was any change in the share market due to his sickness or if the rate of Reliance's shares got affected!

The huge thorn which pricked him more than his physical illness was the rumors his enemies spread about him and Reliance. They spread several false news that Ambani can never get up again and Reliance was planned to be closed down.

Should we especially mention about the speed a rumor can spread? Ambani was worried that if the public believed the rumors, Reliance's shares will be affected, and if that happened, all his investors will be punished.

So, the first task Ambani did once he got better was to invite media people and his primary investors for a meeting and talked to them. 'There is nothing wrong with me. I am fine. I am going abroad for a few tests and will return with the same energy' he promised them with a beaming smile. The news was published in the next day's newspapers and only then Reliance's investors released their bated breath!

Another wise move done by Ambani in that situation was to call his sons, Mukesh and Anil Ambani and share Reliance's responsibilities among them!

Mukesh and Anil were not even thirty years old then. Yet, Dhirubhai Ambani had confidence in their skills. He informed them, 'I am not sure for how long these medical procedures might last. Take care of the company until I return'. Only after getting their confirmation, he submitted himself to the doctors!

Ambani used to split successful people into two – Moon people and Sun people!

The moon reflects the light which it absorbs from the sun as its own. Although it shines brightly in the sky, none of its light belongs to the moon – everything is borrowed from the sun!

Likewise, some people enter into the family business which gets passed on to them by their fathers or grandfathers and enjoy the popularity which is not theirs. Ambani called those people 'Moon people'!

There is no pride in being a moon person. The person can bask in the temporary glow until they get to know about the business. But soon they have to get away from it and forge their own path. Only when they start to create their own glory, true success and pride can be felt. Ambani said this to all the 'heir' industrialists whom he met!

Ambani's sons also entered into their father's business. But, due to an unexpected accident, they got a chance to shine as the sun people. They utilized that opportunity and shone well!

Mukesh Ambani took charge of the important responsibility of maintaining and implementing several projects that Reliance was involved in. Anil Ambani took charge of gathering the funds required for investments, marketing, advertisements and other public relations duties.

Both the brothers worked hard under the guidance of Dhirubhai Ambani.

Unlike the expectations of Ambani's enemies, Reliance did not fall. Reliance's wheel started to run with a huge sigh and a prayer for Ambani to get well soon!

***

While Dhirubhai Ambani was under medical treatment and while his two sons took the responsibility of running Reliance, we shall learn more about Ambani's daughters.

There is no news about Ambani's daughters, Nina and Deepti who were born between Mukesh and Anil to have participated in the daily running of the company. But, they both married India's leading entrepreneurs.

Deepti, who loved and married Raj Salgaocar who was well known by Ambani's family since his childhood lives in Goa now. Her sister Nina married Shyam Kothari who belonged in Chennai and moved to Tamilnadu.

While Ambani's sons-in-law belonged to the industrial world, his daughters-in-law belonged to the art world. Mukesh's wife Nita was a school teacher who was proficient in dance and Anil's wife Tina Munim was an actress.

They all live as a joint family in Mumbai. It is a huge family with sons, daughters-in-law and grandchildren!

Dhirubhai Ambani's illness shook the entire family. His entire family stood by him with prayers for him to get well soon.

***

Due to the unexpected cardiac stroke, the right side of body was severely paralyzed. Especially, his right hand.

The world's best doctors treated him first in India and later in Switzerland and the US's California state. Due to their continuous treatments and care, Ambani's health improved slowly.

Apart from the doctors' skills and prayers of numerous families in India, if there would have been another factor that accelerated his recovery, that would have been the telephonic calls and letters that came from India at a regular interval!

They all contained the satiating information that his brainchild Reliance was running smoothly without any issues and they were under safe hands!

A grandfather who is on his deathbed will sprint up with boosted energy when his granddaughter gets married. Just like that positive news about Reliance boosted Ambani's recovery and he regained his original composure soon!

Despite his recovery, according to the doctors' advice, he was supposed to take a rest. Moreover, doctors announced that he had to undergo different kinds of therapy to repair the various body parts which were paralyzed, to their original condition. Only after that, he could return to his office!

Ambani who was active throughout the day should have found the new confinement for months a burden initially. But he found a few exciting moments during then – he spent most of his time playing with his grandson and pampering him!

Dhirubhai Ambani was able to go back to his office and resume his responsibilities only in 1989. Until then, his sons managed the company on his behalf. Since Ambani's opinion was asked in the major issues, Reliance operated without any major hitches even during his absence!

As we have read earlier, Reliance started manufacturing a chemical substance called PTA in its Patalganga industry in 1986. From 1988, it started to manufacture its raw materials named Paraxylene and other substances. Reliance grew into the biggest manufacturer in the Indian chemical industry through these products!

The Fourth World Cup Cricket was conducted in India and Pakistan in 1987. It was a major cricket festival where all the major cricket-playing countries took part. Moreover, the previous World Cup (1983) was won by the Indian cricket team led by Kapil Dev, hence, cricket fans were eagerly looking for the event!

There is no connection between cricket and Reliance. Yet, Reliance considered the World Cup as a good advertising opportunity to reach more people. Reliance is the pioneer for all the advertisers who sell everything ranging from slate pencil to cars using cricket!

The 1987 World Cup series started with Reliance as its primary sponsor. Since the trophy was also termed as 'Reliance Cup', Reliance's name had an excellent reach all over the world!

Everybody expected India and Pakistan to contest against each other in the final match since they conducted the match, but Australia won that 'Reliance Cup'. Nevertheless, Reliance won a huge profit due to the match series!

In general, although sponsors get huge fame and name by sponsoring such sports events, while looking at the monetary benefit there would be none. But Reliance showcased a unique approach and utilized the name and fame received from the 'Reliance Cup' cricket match to improve its business further and increased its profit!

***

The popular Larsen and Turbo (L&T) company faced a huge crisis in the year 1988. It was gravely affected and it could survive only if somebody resurrects the company!

Ambani developed an interest in L&T then. Since he was always liked to tinker with new things, he started to think about buying L&T at a cheaper price while it was available!

Moreover, L&T's then chairperson had huge respect for Ambani. He believed that Ambani can turn hay into gold and he surrendered his entire support to Ambani saying, 'Only you can save L&T from ulterior destruction and resurrect it to its original glory!'

Ambani's sons took charge as the directors of L&T company. Ambani returned from long rest in 1989 and became the President of L&T!

Everybody who looked at Ambani who overcame two menacing demons - stroke and paralysis were stunned. The reason was that there was not even a shadow of tiredness or fatigue on Ambani. He started to function again with the same energy as if he just awoke from his sleep!

In truth, Ambani's paralysis had prevented a few of his body parts to function with the same force as before. But, Ambani utilized his sharp brain skills to never reveal his weakness and functioned effectively. Ambani's close acquaintances say that his actions had vigor and speed to achieve what could not do for the previous three years.

Ambani balanced himself successfully on two fast-pacing horses – Reliance and L&T. Yet, another trial waited for him at the end of 1989. His former 'foe' VP Singh became the Prime Minister of India!

Ambani's other adversary, The Indian Express also entered the opposition field with full speed. Indian Express researched and wrote that several misconducts were done in the purchase of L&T's shares by Ambani. Ambani vehemently refused the claim.

The matter went to court when the situation could not be trusted enough. Ambani was forced to surrender the shares he purchased, in the end. He faced a huge loss due to it. He was forced to resign his post as President of L&T!

***

Apart from these ripples, Reliance company continued to thrive with stable growth and profits. Mukesh Ambani and Anil Ambani successfully ran the company with the guidance of Dhirubhai Ambani.

Statistics can be quoted to explain the growth achieved by Reliance under young Ambani's rein. When Ambani faced a cardiac stroke in 1986, Reliance company's total value was around a thousand crores. In the next fifteen years, while everybody was criticizing that Ambani was in his full form, Reliance's worth has increased 160 times!

Ambani and his sons' hard work, planning and responsibility-sharing were behind the tremendous growth of Reliance. Mukesh Ambani and Anil Ambani took charge of Reliance during a difficult period. Everybody was closely monitoring the brothers to check if they were capable of withholding their father's empire or if they might fail.

Despite a person's skills, a small tremor is expected under such scrutiny. But, thankfully, senior Ambani's experience saved Mukesh and Anil. Although he was under continuous medical care, his decision was final in all the critical problems and policy decisions of Reliance. Mukesh Ambani and Anil Ambani were able to thrive under his direction!

The good thing that happened amidst all the commotion was that the skilled brothers Mukesh and Anil took it as an opportunity to showcase their talents. They believed that their talents can be proved by running the company with the same speed as their father. They both strived hard and achieved success in their mission. As a result, both of them individually became successful entrepreneurs. The 'Business India' magazine commemorated Mukesh Ambani-Anil Ambani brothers with their 'Best Indian Entrepreneurs' award in 1997.

While Ambani's enemies falsely campaigned that Reliance is Ambani and when Ambani goes down the company also would go down, Ambani looked upon his sons running the company with maturity with pride! In that satisfaction, he mentioned, "Reliance will thrive with or without me!"

"It is true that I created and reared Reliance. But now it has grown from an industrial company into a policy group. An individual has no specific importance here. Dhirubhai Ambani is here today and he might go tomorrow. But Reliance's employees and shareholders will always make the company thrive."

***

The next step in Reliance's evolutionary growth brought Ambani's long-term dream to come true. It was the project to make a person who once filled petrol to vehicles in Yeden into an emperor of the Indian petroleum industry!

❑❑❑

Chapter 10

We are looking in detail at the successful entrepreneur Dhirubhai Ambani. It is difficult to separate Ambani from his businesses. Yet, if we learn about his interests, hobbies and other details, it would be easy for us to have an image of him.

Ambani had sparkling dark eyes. His specific identification traits were a smiling face, sharp vision and a fit body.

Although Ambani was known as a serious businessman, he was entirely a different person when he spent time with his friends. Once business talks were done with his professional friends, he had the habit of talking jovially to them. On hearing good humor, he used to laugh out loud!

He would do anything for his friends. He treated friendship with dignity.

He was not interested in politics. But he used to know about the results in all the constituencies during elections. He liked to watch Gujarati dramas!

He was a 'Paan' fan. He had the habit of munching 12 paans at the office and 12 at home!

He liked children a lot. He wanted to raise children according to our Indian culture. Ambani appointed a separate teacher to teach his grandchildren about the bravery of the Shivaji, Jhansi ki Rani and other great Indian.

Ambani used to walk and exercise on a daily basis, weekly went for mountain climbing and preferred to keep his body fit. He had a private gym inside his house for it.

His favorite car was a white Cadillac and his favorite cuisine was Gujarati.

***

Let us come back to the Reliance office now. Everybody was talking about 'ICPL'. What is that ICPL? Why are they arguing about it?

Until the first half of the nineties, the Indian Petroleum industry was under the control of a government agency named ICPL – Indian PetroChemical Limited!

The petroleum industry includes not only the petrol bunks at our street end, it involves a variety of associate businesses. The chemicals obtained from crude petroleum are used as a raw material in several industries including plastic and textiles. Hence, petroleum chemicals had a huge need in India whose industrial growth was tremendous.

Just like there is just a single sun and a single moon for the entire earth, ICPL had the monopoly for all the petrochemical products all over India. ICPL ruled all the small and large entrepreneurs with tight control.

But the irony was that petroleum products manufactured in the three factories of ICPL were able to meet only half of India's total needs. The rest of the products were imported from foreign countries. Yet, ICPL had great respect in the field as there was nobody to compete with them then. ICPL was one of the most profitable government companies of that period!

During several situations, ICPL had not been able to manufacture enough petrochemical products to meet the needs. Yet, just like our ration shops, businessmen had to take what was available and continue their production.

Due to several reasons like this, there was a need for an alternative to ICPL. Many had the impression that if only there is a competition ICPL would perform better!

At that time, Reliance company which was involved in the manufacture of textiles and chemicals related to it started to think about stepping into the petroleum industry.

Ambani and his sons chose Hazira in Gujarat as their location and started to build a huge petrochemical industry.

Hazira was barren land. Reliance faced several obstacles in refining the place and constructing the factory. The Government did not provide any facility which they had promised before. The water was not good, electricity was not enough, there were no harbor facilities to bring the instruments needed for the factory and so on.

But, Ambani did not allow his dreams to turn into dust due to such problems. He made all the facilities needed for the construction of the Hazira plant including roadways, seaways and other amenities at his own cost!

Although it cost a lot to Reliance, Ambani's plan was fulfilled without any issues. Moreover, Ambani had an additional benefit in it. Instead of depending upon the government for all the facilities, if the industries started to fulfil their own needs, the industrial location will improve and they can be self-sufficient. Ambani was a pioneer of the industrialist self-sufficiency.

It started with Narida, Patalganga and extended till Hazira and later Jamnagar. Reliance adopted all the places where its industries were located and provided all the facilities including schools, hospitals, water and transport. Due to this, not only Reliance employees, but everybody benefited from it.

The major reason for the construction of the Hazira plant was to produce all the petrochemical products needed for Reliance's Patalganga plant. Ambani planned to sell the excess products to the rest of the plastic and textile industries.

We mention it as Hazira plant as a singular entity for our convenience. But, in reality, it compromised several plants which were built at international standards. Poly-ethylene, poly-propylene, poly vinyl chloride known as PVC, PFY, PSF, PTA, polyester terephthalate, mono ethylene glycol and several chemical substances can be manufactured in those plants. Reliance's Hazira plant was one of the largest plants in the entire world.

Ambani constructed the Hazira plant with the latest technology and with all the facilities as usual. But, when the products manufactured in those plants reached the market for sales, Reliance faced a lot of obstacles.

The petroleum industry was down all over the world at that time. Hence, the rate of petrochemical products was at its lowest. Moreover, Reliance had to face competition from the expert of the industry, ICPL.

But Dhirubhai Ambani did not fret about the obstacles. He believed wholeheartedly that the need for petrochemical products will exponentially increase in the next four or five years. He predicted that all the companies will struggle to manage the increased demand then!

With that expectation, Ambani invested a huge amount in his Hazira plant and built it with precision. 'Reliance Petroleum' shares were released in 1993 for this and they were sold immediately.

During this period, Ambani's other dream got fulfilled. Reliance traded for more than 4000 crores in the year 1993 and received the honor 'India's largest private company'!

Following that, in 1995, Reliance got a profit of more than a thousand crores – which was an achievement that no other private company had even dreamed of!

***

The Hazira plant's construction which went at a slow pace finally got completed in 1996-97. It stood proud as the biggest chemical plant in Asia with a worth of around nine thousand crores!

Ambani's prediction that the need for petrochemical products would increase in the next five years came true. Since Hazira started to function at its full capacity by then, Reliance reaped the results of that 'sudden demand'!

When compared to Ambani's other ventures, his growth in the petrochemical industry was slow. But, once Ambani experienced the huge profit from this opportunity, he utilized the industry and developed his business!

Within five years of entering the petrochemical field, Reliance overtook the experienced ICPL and became the number 1 petrochemical company in India!

The next feather on Ambani's hat is that Reliance engulfed its major competitor ICPL in the next five years. Reliance bought 26 percent shares of ICPL in 2002 and with that Reliance became the quarter owner of the government company!

***

Ambani prepared himself for the next project once he imprinted his name deeply in the petrochemical industry.

His next dream was to establish an oil refinery plant with international standards!

He chose a place named Jamnagar in Gujarat for the project. Just like any other 'Ambani' way, a huge plant with a huge investment, advanced technology and facilities everything was in place!

Just like in Hazira, Reliance did not expect government aids in Jamnagar. It created everything ranging from power supply to the seawater purification plant needed for the plant by itself. On the whole, Reliance invested 25,000 crores in the plant. No other plant in India has been constructed at such a budget so far!

We might be astonished at the cost of constructing the Jamnagar plant. But, when compared to the cost involved in building an oil refining plant in other countries, Ambani and his sons completed the Jamnagar plant at a lower cost – within three years – This was considered a world record!

When the construction of the Jamnagar plant which started in 1997, spreading over 21 sq. kilometers completed in 1999-2000, it bagged the honor of the biggest oil purification plant in India. Petroleum experts rated the Jamnagar plant as one of the best plants in the entire world!

Once the Jamnagar plant started to operate at its full capacity, Reliance's other four plants also contributed to its growth. Since Reliance manufactured all the raw materials needed for the manufacture of its textiles through its four plants, production cost was reduced to a great extent. Moreover, since they were able to confirm the quality of each raw material, Reliance clothing's quality increased as a whole!

In short, quality clothing at a lower cost and no need to depend on anybody for anything. This self-sufficiency was achieved through the Jamnagar plant!

The huge and efficient Jamnagar plant fulfilled twenty-five percent of India's total need in the oil refining industry. This revived India's oil industry. India which was importing diesel before started to export diesel to other countries.

Apart from these achievements, the Jamnagar plant holds another importance. It was the plant that completed Reliance's growth. Jamnagar plant's success made Ambani's dream of becoming the all-rounder in everything ranging from the petroleum industry to textiles come true!

Let us look at Ambani's business empire from a bird's view at this point.

Crude petroleum is being refined at Ambani's 'new' Jamnagar plant. We carry the raw material produced there to Hazira. Several petrochemical products are manufactured using the raw material that we brought. Take those petrochemical products to Patalganga. PSF, PFY and other raw materials needed for the production of polyester are being done there. Let us take those and go to Ambani's first plan in Naroda. They get everything we have and weave them into polyester clothes and give it to us. We happily clad them!

We feel overwhelmed by just reading and writing about it. But all these were made possible through the ever-tiring hard work of a single person. While realizing the enormity of his achievement, Dhirubhai Ambani's famous quote comes to our mind:

'Do your work with unrelenting confidence and skill. Success will find its way to you!'

Chapter 11

Yeden received seventeen-year-old Ambani with welcoming hands, employed him and supported him. Five decades since his return to his homeland, 'Aden' bagged the world's accolades to his Reliance company!

The company started by Ambani along with Chambaklal Damani in 1959, after returning from Yeden was called 'Reliance Commercial Corporation'.

Ambani who was doing only commercial business as per his company's name until 1966, entered into textile manufacture by building a separate spinning mill. Since then, his companies were called 'Reliance Industries Limited' or in short as 'RIL'.

Later, he entered petroleum industry in 1991. He formed a sister concern named Reliance Petroleum Limited – RPL!

RIL and RPL both grew in their fields with infinite successes. Since RPL's products were the major raw materials for RIL, both RIL and RPL had a good trade relationship with each other. They both operated as separate entities in the share market as well.

Within 2001, both RIL and RPL have grown into huge groups. Ambani considered merging both and forming a mega-company then!

The name chosen by him for that 'Mega' project was Project Aden!

The first step of the merger was to explain to Reliance's investors and employees about the need for it and to get their approval. Both the companies were not private property. Lakhs of common people have invested in them through the share market. Only if a majority of those 'small owners' approve of the project, both the companies could be merged!

But there was no major hiccup for the project. Detailed reports were released by Reliance about the economic benefits that would happen to Reliance and its investors. People believed Ambani as usual and welcomed the merger with their open hearts.

In 2002, RIL and RPL merged to form the 'Reliance'. This was celebrated as the biggest merger in the Indian industrial world. Ambani received several accolades for the merger – both local and international!

Reliance which was already the biggest private company in India grew bigger after the merger. The 'new' company had assets worth sixty thousand crores. Thirty-five lakh Indians were its investors – it was the third biggest investors family in the world!

'Fortune' business magazine selects the world's 500 best companies each year as 'Fortune 500'. This list is popular among those in the industrial world. Being a part of that list is not an ordinary feat. Only those companies which excel in all categories earn a huge profit and which has all the plans in place can enter into Fortune's list!

Companies that find a way into the Fortune list, proudly brag that they are a 'Fortune 500 company'. Until the year 2002, no private Indian firm managed to get that honor!

In such a situation, integrated Reliance bagged the 412th place in 2002's Fortune list. Reliance got the honor of the 'First Indian Fortune 500 private company'!

While Reliance was honored with Fortune, Ambani too was showered with appreciations and accolades. Magazines and industrial groups praised him as the best industrialist of the twentieth century!

If you have any concerns, look at the gist of awards and recognitions that Ambani got during the nineties and later:

Chemtech company's "Best man of the century" award, praising him for the work he has done for the growth of India's chemical industry (November 2000).

'Best Indian Entrepreneur' award given by Federation of Indian Chambers of Commerce and Industries (FICCI)

(March 2000- The award was given by US President Bill Clinton).

'Lifetime Achiever' award given by Indian Human Resource Development (HRD Congress) (February 2002).

Award and shield gave by Mumbai Greater City Corporation appreciating Ambani's contribution to the growth of Greater Mumbai (December 2000).

'Lifetime Achiever' award given by 'Economic Times' magazine commemorating Ambani for his contribution toward the growth of private companies in India and overall industrial growth (August 2001 – Ambani dedicated this award to the whole of the Reliance family).

'Outstanding Visionary of the Twentieth Century' award given by Indian Merchants Chamber for Ambani's achievements in the industrial and investment industry (December 1999).

First place in the internet poll 'Best Indian entrepreneur of the twentieth century' conducted by 'Business Barons' magazine. (August – October 1999).

"Best Indian of the Twentieth Century" honor in the industrial category in the internet polls conducted by 'Times of India' (January 2000 – Indians who got this honor in other categories: Mahatma Gandhi in the 'Leaders and Politicians', Swami Vivekananda in the 'Spiritual philosophers' category and Lata Mangeshkar 'Achievers in Art' category).

Special badge given by Wharton Institutions/ Pennsylvania University honoring Ambani's leadership qualities toward other budding entrepreneurs (June 1998 – Ambani was the first Indian to get the badge).

Honorary Member post given by England's Textile Institute honoring Ambani's innovations in textiles and to attract others into the industry (1994).

Ambani was chosen three times for the 'Asia's fifty bigshots' list published by 'Asia Week' magazine (2000, 1998 & 1996).

He was chosen as the most respected Indian in the polls conducted by Zee TV and Earnst & Young company (January 2000).

Ambani had a special mention as the one who modernized the Indian share market in the special list published by 'India Today' weekly magazine under the topic '100 people who sculpted India in the twentieth century' (January 2000).

The only Indian who found a place in the 'Best Entrepreneurs' list released by 'Asia Week' magazine (October 1998).

'Asia's promising star' honor given by US's 'Business Week' magazine (June 1998).

As mentioned before, this is just a shortened version. Ambani has accumulated numerous awards and recognitions over the years!

More than these awards, Ambani considered the Indian youngsters who were inspired by his successes and indulged themselves in self-employment considering him as their role models to the be the real achievement that he has accomplished. Ambani is considered a psychological guru for a generation.

Even today, the goal of each Indian who starts a business will be 'I will grow big and achieve as Ambani did'!

Ambani wanted that to happen. He strongly believed that industrial growth will be the backbone of a nation's growth. He used to repeat frequently that India needs many such active youngsters. His belief and hope were that those youngsters had the possibility of making India an economic superpower on the international stage!

Ambani mentioned during a magazine's interview, "If I can do so much for the Indian industrial world, just think about our industrial wealth if there are a thousand such Ambanis!" He believed that finding a thousand Ambanis is not a tough task at all.

Ambani's Indian dream was 'thousands of Indian youngsters are waiting with big dreams and higher goals. If they all get good opportunities, work hard to reach their goals, the Indian industrial world will grow on par with the rest of the world very soon!'

Ambani made sure that all his dreams were achieved through his efforts. We all have to work together to achieve his Indian dream!

Only then, 'Ambani's achievement list' will get completed!

❑❑❑

Chapter 12

Dhirubhai Ambani is respected as the most important achiever in Independent India. Ambani and his innovative attempts are the backbones of the growth which India has achieved in the industrial world. He was the one who regulated the Indian share market which was running haphazardly before his arrival!

Ambani started the 'Reliance' company from scratch and through his steadfast hard work he reached a successful peak within twenty-five years which many multigenerational companies have never dreamed of. Nobody can deny his success – due to this fact, even his enemies respect Ambani!

Former President of India K. R. Narayanan has mentioned that Ambani was an exemplary person and has said, 'We all have to observe and study his life'.

Why should we study it? Only when we observe Ambani's successful life, his 'success formula' which is scattered all over the years can be found.

Everybody starts some business. But, if Ambani can reach such a height, what is the magic behind it?

There is no magic, but only a few easy steps behind the success. If one respects and follows it, even you and I can become a mini Ambani!

You cannot read those steps in any business self-help books. But all these are proven to be successful. The person who realized its importance and followed them has created the largest private business empire in India!

If you are suffering from poverty, do not fret about it and find a way to come out of it. After that, it will not hinder you.

Ambani was born in a poor family. Was not educated well. All those facts did not create an inferiority complex in him, but, the struggles he faced while poor triggered him and improved him!

In whatever field we may indulge in, we should develop our knowledge superior to those others in the same field!

Ambani entered the textile industry without any experience. But he read several books regarding textile manufacture, discussed with various merchants, analyzed various kinds of clothing and found the differences between them and developed his knowledge about the industry within a short duration. After that, he was able to find the quality of fibers by hearing the sound of its slipping!

Instead of concentrating only on the matters which directly involve you, watch your surroundings and observe what happens around you!

American leader Dr. Henry Kissinger who visited India met Ambani. Later, he appreciated Ambani's knowledge about world trade!

Not only him, all those who were acquainted with Ambani wondered about his worldly knowledge. They say that Ambani kept information such as the new changes, technologies, innovation and economic problems in the industrial world of both India and the world!

Ambani utilized this knowledge and when came across new opportunities, he grabbed them immediately!

Curiosity and courage are needed to involve in a new venture. Strength is also needed to lose a few comforts for that new venture!

Ambani had a stable job with a good salary in Yeden. What induced him to return to India, invest his life's savings, start a new business and struggle with that? How did he bear the discomforts of seven members living in a place which is big enough only for three members?

The only answer to all these questions is his courage. No discomfort bothered him during his journey to reach his goal! This strength and courage are the basic needs of those who involve in trade!

'Do big' Whatever you plan to do, do it big!

Ambani's factories were big when compared to the other factories in the same field. Since he planned for larger production, he was able to reduce the production cost and was able to sell his products at a lower rate. At the same time, such measures were needed for the country's industrial growth.

For example, when Ambani started Polyester production, he constructed his production plant which was big enough to produce ten thousand tons of products per year. Provisions were made to expand the same plant to produce fifteen tons of products. The important thing to be noted here was that India's total Polyester sale was just six thousand tons per year at that time!

"There is nothing that we cannot do. We have to try everything!"

Ambani's confidence raised him from the 'merchant' level to the 'entrepreneur' level. In the year 1965, Ambani's partner during that time, Chambaklal Damani opposed his entry into the clothing manufacturing business. Ambani ignored his partner's doubts and started his spinning mill with confidence. The world knows what happened next!

Likewise, when he chose Jamnagar for his oil refinery plant, he approached a private consulting agency to analyze the place. They inspected Jamnagar and reported that there are no facilities to start and run a plant in Jamnagar.

But, Ambani trusted his instincts more than the report provided by them. Since he wanted to do and excel in something that was declared impossible, the Jamnagar plant work was continued amidst so many discomforts. Today, the Jamnagar Reliance plant is one of the largest oil refineries in the world and stands as proof of Ambani's self-confidence!

If you want to do business in India, the management lessons you learned in your textbooks will not help you. The rules are different here and you have to bend yourselves according to the rules!

This was the important advice given by Ambani to those who completed their MBA abroad and wanted to start a business in India – Forget what you learned in your textbooks. The rules and tricks to run a business in different here, learn them and act accordingly!

Reliance company grew steadily even during the 'License Raj' period where strict rules were prevalent. Now, the situation is the exact opposite due to globalization and Reliance's success continues. The major factor for this is that Ambani understood the Indian industrial market and ran his industry with timely changes!

Foresight is necessary. We have to think about the future now itself!

Ambani's popular Backward Integration policy can be quoted as an example here. While he was occupied in clothing manufacture and everything was progressing toward success, he was able to think "why don't we manufacture the raw materials needed for it?". He was able to imagine his own oil refinery while he was an apprentice in the petrochemical industry. His foresight took him to greater heights in each step!

Dream about your goals. Dreams should not be simple, dream big!

As our Indian President A.P.J. Abdul Kalam has quoted, Ambani had 'Dream big' as his life's message. He believed that only those who dream can make it happen in real life!

It might be fun to read, but an important truth is hidden here. If a person is hesitant to imagine himself as a great singer, it means that he lacks confidence in his skills. How can he achieve something if he lacks confidence in his own skills?

The major trigger for all of Ambani's successes was his dreams. He dreamed about many things which many were not even aware of and spent his entire life bringing them to reality!

Be pleasant and attract everybody!

All those who were acquainted with Ambani say this without fail – A smiling face, bright eyes, sharp vision, the caring way he speaks to the other person, infinite knowledge, the care which he employs while talking to anybody, listening to the other person's view without interfering and quick thinking are his plus points!

In short, Ambani found a place in anybody's heart whom he spoke to. Due to this nature, he had the support and love of many in both business and personal circles!

Likewise, Ambani was known for the care he showed to ordinary employees like peons and clerks in his office!

People who work along with you are very important for your success. Hence, choose them with care and handle them with caution!

Ambani took great care in selecting his employees. His policy was to choose the most talented ones for the job without considering his personal opinion on the person!

Due to this behavior, Ambani had an efficient workforce. He was proud of his workforce too!

If choosing talented people is important, how to treat them and how to handle them is more important. Ambani did well in that aspect too!

Ambani was never into micromanaging his employees. Once he chose a person, he never wanted to tie them up with petty instructions. He trusted his employees and hence gave them complete freedom. Employees were happy with their independence and performed their tasks with more interest and happiness. Reliance's total production also increased!

Talk less and show your talents in action!

Ambani is the real-life example for 'Karma Yogi' from Bhagavad Gita. He often told his friends, "we will do it, we have to do it" – since he followed this quote to its full extent, Reliance empire stands as the testimony of his forty-year-old hard work.

There is no use in fretting over something that we do not have. If that skill is needed for our business, learn it at any cost. If you feel that you can manage fine without it, then do not agonize about it!

Ambani's English knowledge was average. He was able to convey what he wanted to convey without any issues. But grammatical errors and stutters happened at times.

Once, his friend Murli Deora's son made fun of Ambani's broken English!

Ambani did not show any embarrassment over his shortcoming, he replied to him, "Speaking English without any errors is a skill, running a business and earning money is another skill. I have all the skills needed to run my business and I am satisfied with that!"

Reduce production cost, increase production quality – profit will automatically increase!

Ambani's successful trade secret since he entered textile manufacture till today's Reliance India Mobile is the same – reduce the cost and price for the manufacture of a product. At the same time, increase the production quantity and increase the profit too!

For example, consider a pen of good quality available in the market for ten rupees. The production cost of a pen might be eight and a half rupees. Consider we sell lakh pens in a month and selling a pen at a profit of one and a half rupees yields us one and a half lakhs rupees as profit!

Now, with a few cost-cutting measures, let us manufacture the pen at eight rupees and sell them at nine rupees each. Our profit will decrease from one and a half rupees to one rupee. But, when a ten rupees' pen is available at eight rupees, more buyers prefer our pen. So, we can sell two lakh pens per month which will earn us two lakh rupees a month – the profit increases by fifty thousand!

Replace pens with clothing materials, artificial fibers, chemical substances and petroleum products. We can decipher Ambani's trade secrets!

High quality always –no compromise in it!

Just because it was sold at a lower cost, Ambani's products are not of low-quality. Ambani did no compromise on the quality of his products.

All the industries built by Ambani were constructed at an international standard which even foreigners were stunned to look at. Ambani made sure of his products' high standards through advanced technology, high quality raw materials and flawless products. Due to these reasons, Reliance products are being exported to several world nations!

Whatever the business may be, its real success lays in the goodness we do for the public.

Ambani often said that keeping the public happy is very important for a business. They buy your products, and if they are not happy, you have to fall, no matter what height you have reached!

Since Ambani believed this rule, he worked keeping his customers' and investors' benefit in mind. People continued to support him in turn!

No need to lust for foreign funds. Instead of living on their investment, have confidence that we can do it for ourselves!

Indian industries get investment from foreign countries and expand themselves. Ambani strongly held his stand that Reliance will never do that!

'We can purchase the required technology from them. If needed, we can obtain a loan from foreign nations. But we should never lower our standard and permit them to invest in our companies. This was Ambani's policy!

At the same time, he believed that instead of importing foreign goods and selling them here, it is better to produce those products in India. Due to this, unwanted imports will be reduced and our nation's industrial wealth will be increased. Moreover, if they can do it, why can we not?

Completing a task at the given time and the given cost will increase the trust in your business.

Although Ambani was educated only till the tenth standard, he was a good manager when he entered the business world. His unique feature was to complete all the new projects that he has undertaken at the committed time within the accepted budget. There was not even a day's delay or an excess penny spent!

He used to say to his co-workers, "Completing a task at the stipulated time is important. But, at the same time, if the task is completed before the deadline, I will be happier!"

Discuss with everybody without bothering about their status. You will get more information and support from them.

When Ambani was once asked, "How do you decide to involve or not to involve in a business?" He replied, "I will ask my driver and decide!"

It was not for fun. That was the truth. Ambani used to talk and discuss with his driver, assistant, gardener, maids and all the common people whom he met every day and get their views. This habit helped him to know what is the demand for a particular product in the market and what do people think about it!

There is no use in wanting to do everything by yourself – share your workload with your co-workers and trust them to complete it successfully!

Ambani had a heart stroke in the year 1986. Until then, he was the one who was involved in all the major decisions involving Reliance. But doctors had put a barrier to continue doing the same!

So, Ambani did not hesitate further and shared the responsibilities between his two sons. Ambani's trust in those young talents sculpted Reliance's growth for the next fifteen years!

Good friends and relations are very important for our success, safeguard them always!

Once, Ambani's business acquaintance visited him in Mumbai. Ambani promised to send his car to the railway station and welcome him!

But, due to some other crisis, the car could not reach the railway station at the right time.

The acquaintance did not mind the miss but Ambani was ashamed by it. He felt bad that he was not able to keep up his promise to his friend.

To compensate for his 'mistake', Ambani sent his friend in his luxury car to look around Mumbai. Only after completing that 'sudden' tour they met and started to discuss their businesses!

Ambani did anything and everything possible for his business and personal friends, and his friends believed him so!

Not only friends, don't forget your enemies too!

Anybody who once gets acquainted with Ambani cannot forget him easily. Everybody is familiar with the affection Ambani shows to his friends. But, the one important matter which many were not aware of it was that he remembered his enemies and protestors too!

A small incident can be quoted as an example of Ambani's memory. When Reliance entered the share market, its annual meetings were conducted on huge grounds in front of thousands of its investors. Despite the huge crowd, Ambani never failed to identify those people whom he knew well.

In one such meeting, a person threw a wicked question at Ambani. The question was intended to embarrass Ambani and Reliance.

Ambani who was talking before the crowd looked at the person amidst the crowd. He identified the person in the middle of so many faces and recalled information about him. When Ambani started to say details about him, the prankster was stupefied!

You have to answer fair feedbacks. But, keep silent for those unfair accusations!

During media interviews, even though Ambani did not approve the comments and feedback put forth before him, he answered all the questions properly.

But, at one period, when the magazines started to shower negative news and innumerable accusations toward him, Ambani understood that his time was getting wasted in answering them. He did not talk to any media person after that!

He used to say, "I am not worried about those who throw accusations on me. My skin is tough, hence, those arrows cannot pierce me". Due to this attitude, no complaint bothered him much. He believed in the proverb that only the tree that bears fruits will get stoned and continued to focus on his company's growth!

Patience, at times, is a virtue!

Ambani was active by nature. He could not stay at the same place for long. In whatever venture he gets involved he wanted it to bear fruits immediately. He wanted the saplings he planted in the morning to bear flowers in the evening!

But the Indian industrial world was a direct inverse of him. He struggled a lot during his initial stages not being able to bear the turtle speed of the Indian government!

Hence, he started to compensate the government's delay by completing the tasks from his side earlier and quickly. That is if he knew that government takes ten days to approve something, he sent the application ten days before the intended date and he concentrated on other tasks until the approval comes in!

Reinvest the profit you got in the business here itself. It will multiply further!

When Ambani earned some profit in the Polyester production, he did not turn toward movie production. He reinvested all the profits earned in the business world into the same field and reaped huge profits!

Just because we earn well does not mean that we have to spend a lot!

Even after accumulating wealth for the next few generations, Ambani did not allow unwanted expenditures or luxuries. He did not forego his simple lifestyle – although he stayed in five-star hotels, he ate in the nearby canteens!

Do not forget your roots despite the heights you reach, do something for those who did something for you!

Ambani who was born in Gujarat – Sourashtra made his living in Yeden at first and at Mumbai later. But his heart was still at his roots!

He visited his native place at times and spent time with his childhood friends. He celebrated birthdays and other celebrations with his native people which made him the son of his soil!

Ambani wanted the villages, Chorwad and Kukasvada where he was born and brought up, to get all the basic needs and to become model villages in India. It is known that he has spent 25 lakhs per year on these two villages to provide them drinking water, schools and hospitals.

Anyone who came to Mumbai from these two villages was able to meet and talk to Ambani easily. Ambani did everything for their families. Many youngsters from those villages got jobs in Reliance. He helped a few of them to study abroad and did many other good deeds.

Moreover, Reliance has done 70% of its investments in Gujarat state. This is not just a coincidence; this was Ambani's respect for his home state.

Your success does not belong to you alone.

When Ambani accepted the 'Lifetime Achiever' award given by Economic Times in 2001, he dedicated the award to the entire Reliance family. He said, "On behalf of the thousands of Reliance employees, managers who guide them, friends who support us, and above them all, the investors who have unwavering faith over us, I will accept his award".

Ambani understood that the main contributor to his success was the support given by the Reliance family. He never hesitated to acknowledge that and thank them in public!

Spend your leisure time effectively!

Ambani who was a successful person in the Indian industrial world was not a member of any club or group.

Ambani was clear on this decision – He spent all his leisure time apart from work with his family. He had no time for business groups, committees and others.

Ambani's leisure time was so rare and he preferred to spend it with his family. He went on a long vacation with his family at least once every year. His favorite tourist spot was Munnar (Kerala)

Health matters!

Ambani believed that a healthy body and a happy family are the conforming factors of a person's victory.

Ambani maintained his body fir through daily exercises and a balanced diet. After recovering from cardiac stroke and paralysis in 1986, he was able to return to his normal self and walk without a walking stick!

Need an unsatisfied mind! Only then we can achieve more!

Ambani never had the satisfaction that he has achieved all he has dreamed of. If he had got the satisfaction, he would not have achieved further.

Hence, even after reaching greater heights, he considered himself to be at the start of his journey. He heart believed that 'there is a long way to go' and traveled further in search of more accomplishments.

❏❏❏

Chapter 13

"Do you have any regrets in your successful life? Do you feel that something might have been done differently now?" – this question was asked to Ambani during an interview. His reply was:

"I was completely engulfed in developing my business and Reliance and could not allow much time for social service. I regret that now."

Ambani's response should be considered as an example of his humbleness. The reason is that Ambani has already done many good deeds for this community both personally and through Reliance!

Reliance shares have helped several lakhs of people to improve their economic status. That was a huge social service!

Through the four huge industries Reliance constructed in various fields, several thousand were employed either directly or indirectly. Moreover, through the 'Vimal' sales depots, 'Reliance India Mobile phone' programs, Ambani has created several self-employment opportunities.

Ambani has helped Gujarat and Maharashtra in numerous ways to build educational institutions and hospitals. Reliance themselves are running schools effectively in Naroda, Patalganga, Hazira and Jamnagar where Reliance industries are located. Not only Reliance employees' but other families also benefit from them.

One another service done by Ambani in the educational field is to provide scholarships to students each year. This service is carried out in Gujarat, Maharashtra, Goa, Diu and Daman regions. Two thousand to fifteen thousand rupees are given to the students who get the first three ranks in each district in tenth and twelfth standards.

In 2001, Ambani started a free computer education service in 51 corporation schools. Sixty-eight thousand underprivileged students will be benefited from this project.

The Dhirubhai Ambani Foundation (DAF) founded in 1995 is effectively functioning in the education and medical departments.

This foundation is running two educational institutions at international standards – 'Dhirubhai University' (for Science and Technology studies), 'Dhirubhai Ambani Institute' (for Computer studies) in Gandhinagar.

Apart from these, Ambani has donated forty lakh dollars (around twenty crore rupees in Indian value) to the Wharton Educational Institutions in Pennsylvania. This amount will be used to train those students who want to enter the industrial world with a unique perspective.

During the earthquake which shook India a few years back, Ambani and Reliance company entered the field and rescued many. In a few most affected villages, Reliance employees and rescue team reached before government officials and started their rescue operations!

Reliance adopted a village Anjar which was badly affected by the earthquake. The rescue operation was done at the regular Reliance speed and the village was resurrected within the next fifteen days. Alternate arrangements were made for those who lost their houses and other facilities were also done!

In the report submitted by Norway University on the Gujarat earthquake, it is mentioned, 'If not for Reliance's support, it would have taken a minimum three months for Anjar village to stand up on its feet'. The report commemorates the vigor and speed with which Reliance employees and managers functioned and asks the other rescue group to learn from them!

Likewise, during the Maharashtra floods and Gujarat drought, Reliance officers and workers rushed to their rescue under Ambani's direct command.

***

Ambani believed in God, but not in other formalities like pujas or fasting.

Ambani started all his industries and new ventures only after a formal puja to satisfy his family and others around him. According to him, service to fellow human beings is more divine than the service to God!

Once, Ambani talked to popular Ramayana preacher Rameshbhai Oza. It is said that he told him, 'Why shouldn't your devotees indulge themselves in laying roads, pipes to distribute water and other social services instead of singing devotional songs all day.'

***

Ambani frequently said that he wanted to do something for this country. His achievements in the industrial world and his social services can be added to his achievement list.

❑❑❑

Chapter 14

Ambani is known as a great philosopher along with being a successful businessman. He faced each and every challenge that he met during each stage of his life with confidence, without any negative thoughts and defeated it. Hence, while describing his experiences and thoughts, we can listen to them as a lesson.

Ambani's thoughts and advice which he gave in various situations are compiled here. All of these are said by Dhirubhai Ambani.

Boundless talents are hidden inside each of our youngsters. Encourage them well. Support them completely by creating favorable situations and opportunities for them. Those youngsters will exceed your expectations after that.

I always trust and encourage youngsters – because, they never let me down.

Think big, think quick, always think ahead of your time.

It is best to have your dreams, goals and targets at a reachable distance. After reaching them, you can search for the next goal.

The common things among my past, present and future are relations and trusts. I trusted all those whom I met in this journey and they trusted me back. We both enjoyed good benefits due to this trust.

These relations and trust form the foundation for not only personal relationships but also for the victory of business organizations. The reliable relations we had with investors and customers and the trust which exists between us forms the strong foundation for our company's victory.

Factories and machinery have to be updated regularly – humans too.

Our society hates rich people for some reason. They consider earning money as a sin and consider all those who earn a lot as fraudsters. If this attitude continues, we will always remain poor.

Just like reading a lot and gaining knowledge, earning money is a part of our culture – so, we seek blessings from Lakshmi along with Saraswati.

Big dreams and high goals are necessary. Initiative, interest and hard work to reach those goals are also needed – I expect only these from the Reliance and India.

I want India to become an economic super power and become an immovable bigshot in the whole world. What should we do to achieve that?

First of all, we should understand the problems that we have. More important than that is to find the solutions for them. We have to read more for that – not the text books, but the world market and the innovative ideas and technologies used by the developed countries—the knowledge about them is the first step.

The next step is to respect those who earn a lot.

The third step is to learn to trust – all Indians look at other Indians with a little suspicion – we have to come out of this brainwashed behavior which was created centuries back. We have to trust another Indian.

The most important fourth step – Think big. Think anything at a larger scale and produce big results – there should be no compromise in it!

Do not lose hope in any situation. Despair stops new ventures. Only those who are not confident in their ways find an illegal way. If India has to become a superior nation, we all have to trust others.

We have to look at huge challenges or crises as an opportunity. We should not be scared of it and instead, grab it for our benefit.

Do not quit anything. If you fight with confidence, negative thoughts will go away and success becomes possible.

Never hesitate to try. Our first identity should be our confidence.

Nobody is going to invite you to start a business in a particular field and earn a profit. You have to keep your first step by yourself.

A strong coalition is needed to strengthen India – industrial world, government and society should join together to form that coalition. If all three groups forego their misunderstandings and work together, we can prove our skills to the world. We can cry out load 'India is a land of achievers!'

Our people do not realize their own power. They hide their talents and skills within themselves. If those are brought out, growth and healthy competition will increase and India's economy will surge forward.

All those we have achieved so far have become history now. So, I trust only in the future!

Love only the best. Accept only the best – if a product is not up to your standard, reject it immediately. Do not differentiate it as Indian standard or international standard, if it is not of 'best standard' then reject it!

I never trust in a machine and step into a business. I invest in trusting my employees and people!

An uninhabitable forest. I clean it up and layout platforms to walk in. This is not only for me but for all those who wish to walk this way.

My biggest enemy is the success I have had so far.

I do not believe in Number 1 or Number 2. If I am in the number 1 position, I am happy. I have to do something beyond that for this country.

Do I feel happiness in earning money? – Not really. But I have to earn money at least for the investors who trust in me.

My greatest happiness lies in completing a challenging task. I want to be the first in each task I do.

The price we pay for our success – murmurs, problems and enemies.

Frequently asked question by my friends: "Have you achieved all you have aspired for?"

My never changing my answer for them: No, I have miles to go!

I cannot even imagine retiring from my position. Only if I consider it as a job, then I have to retire from it one day. All I do are happy hobbies. If they do not burden me, why should I retire?

This is my message to all Indian youths: Dream, indulge in your work with confidence. If somebody tries to change you from your decisions, do not yield to them! Do not forget your goals even during your toughest days. Change your obstacles as your stepping stones and climb up. You are sure to win.

Do not worry when oppositions, failures and tough situations attack you. You can dream more only when it is dark. You can make them come true later!

Do you have the guts to dream? If yes, there is a whole world waiting for you to conquer!

❏

Chapter 15

When Ambani's sons, Mukesh and Anil, took responsibility as chief executives, Ambani began to lessen his active working days. He goes to his office only for two to three hours a day, gets involved only in major projects and returns home after he convey his opinion or instructions!

Ambani never dreamed of retiring from his business. Yet, he spent his unexpected leisure time thinking about the well-being of society.

In Ambani's native province, Saurashtra (Gujarat), water scarcity was a long-term problem. He wanted to solve the problem permanently by constructing an enormous dam like the Bhakra Nangal dam.

Another one of his dream projects was to purify the sea water and turn that into drinking water and supply that the water to the people at a low cost. He thought about ways to convert Rajasthan's desert into cultivable lands.

Ambani believed that India's future lies in its agricultural growth. Mukesh Ambani has mentioned that Ambani had wanted to do something for India's agricultural world just like how he had improved India's industrial world.

While Ambani was having several dreams and formulating plans to fulfil them, he suffered another cardiac stroke.

Ambani was his usual happy self at his seventeen floored house 'Sea Wind' in Mumbai on 24th June 2002. Both his sons were at their offices.

Around seven in the evening, Ambani called his assistant and said that he is having some difficulty. Immediately, Ambani's family doctor Sharad Pandey was called for.

When the doctor came and examined Ambani, he was back to his normal self. So, everybody was relaxed and at ease!

But, within the next one hour, Ambani felt the same discomfort again. The situation's severity was understood and he was admitted to the hospital for treatment. He was taken to the popular Breach Candy hospital of Mumbai.

He suffered two more cardiac strokes before reaching the hospital. He was admitted to the ICU in a comatose state and doctors said that he had a brain hemorrhage. Since the central nervous system was affected, all his body functions were affected.

Severe measures were taken to save Ambani under the continuous guidance of expert doctors. Several treatments including electric shock were discussed. There was no improvement in Ambani's health condition even after several attempts.

Ambani's cardia stroke and the following complications raised a huge uproar in the country. Several business tycoons, political leaders, cine stars, artists and the public asked about Ambani's health status through phone and by visiting the Breach Candy hospital. Several prayers were conducted for Ambani's well-being.

Seventy-year-old Ambani's health deteriorated further on July 6 after 13 days of suffering. At the same day, he expired peacefully a few minutes before midnight.

When the news was conveyed to Ambani's wife Kokilaben, she said to her sons with tears clouding her eyes, 'your father went to heaven. That is his eternal residence. God, who sent your father to India to complete a few responsibilities took him back!'

***

Ambani's death shook India. Industrialists were grief stuck that the Indian industrial world has lost one of its major pillars. The public gathered in huge masses around Ambani's house to pay their final respects for the hero who was close to their heart!

Around twenty-five thousand of people participated in the final yatra of Ambani which was done on the next day (July 7, 2002). It was an honor that was available only for the great leaders. Mumbai citizens and out of town people who traveled a long distance tried to witness Ambani's final journey from their terraces, railway station roofs and the tree tops. There was a huge commotion to gather the flowers that fell from the vehicle which carried Ambani!

None of them had ever met Ambani. None has ever talked to him. But, Ambani has made an impact in their lives either directly or indirectly. They wanted to shed tears for such a noble soul.

More than the sad-faced celebrities, the anguish of those no-named, faceless people prove that Ambani has spent his life in a useful manner!

❑❑❑

Chapter 16

Even when Dhirubhai Ambani was fighting for his life in Mumbai's Breach Candy hospital and even when the news spread that he expired on 6th July 2002, Reliance offices and industries continued to operate as usual. Ambani's sons returned to their offices on July 8 itself.

Reliance's circular said, "Dhirubhai Ambani lived and died as a living 'Karmayogi'. The only respect that we can give to him is running his company successfully as usual."

Even now, the Reliance company is growing with the same goal under the leadership of Mukesh Ambani and Anil Ambani. Mukesh Ambani has said in a recent television interview, "We have the responsibility to take Dhirubhai's dreams to the upcoming generations. We will fulfil our father's dream by improving Reliance which has been standing strong for centuries!"

***

Reliance started Ambani's dream project 'Reliance India Mobile' on Ambani's first birthday after his death (December 28, 2002) as a tribute to him. (All the advertisements of this project projected Dhirubhai Ambani. One can learn about his popularity and the regard he had among the public even after his death!)

On the same day, the Central government released a special postal stamp honouring him.

The Indian President A.P.J. Abdul Kalam participated and spoke in the meeting to honour Ambani's first death anniversary on 6th July 2003, "Ambani is an example to prove that those chasing big dreams will succeed in their life". He also quoted two Thirukkurals (Popular couplets in Tamil) as Ambani's life motto:

வெள்ளத்து அனைய மலர்நீட்டம் மாந்தர்தம்

உள்ளத்து அனையது உயர்வு

(We have to believe in ourselves, our growth will be based on that belief – the stem of a flower in a river extends and shrinks according to the water level, and this applies to our growth also)

இடும்பைக்கு இடும்பை படுப்பர் இடும்பைக்கு

இடும்பை படாஅ தவர்.

(Do not let the problems affect you. Instead, find ways to defeat those problems!)

***

The Reliance company which has entered the information technology field through 'Reliance Telecom' and 'Infocom' is now also planning to step into the field of production and distribution of electricity and fuels like petrol and diesel.

Who knows, the next Ambani might emerge from the petrol distribution bunk that the Reliance is planning to start.